THE INVISIBLE WOMAN
IN A RED DRESS

by

Zoe M. McCarthy

THE INVISIBLE WOMAN IN RED DRESS BY ZOE M. MCCARTHY

ISBN: 0-9662499-2-5
Copyright © 2018 by Zoe M. McCarthy
Cover Design by Zoe and John McCarthy

For more information on this book and the author, visit
zoemmccarthy.com

Scripture taken from THE HOLY BIBLE, NEW INTERNATIONAL
VERSION® NIV®
Copyright © 1973, 1978, 1984, 2011 by Biblica, Inc.®. Used by
permission. All rights reserved worldwide.

Library of Congress Cataloging-in-Publication Data
McCarthy, Zoe M.
The Invisible Woman in a Red Dress/ Zoe M. McCarthy 1st ed.

Printed in the United States of America

Praise for Zoe M. McCarthy

"*Gift of the Magpie* is a wonderful read that leaves you wanting to read more."

~Barb Regan on *Gift of the Magpie*

"Zoe M. McCarthy weaves a light, heartwarming read…"

~Toni Shiloh on *Calculated Risk*

"I read this one in one sitting as I could not put it down - I highly recommend this book for anyone who likes reading a sweet and clean romance."

~Dawn Bradman on *Gift of the Magpie*

"I loved this book."

~Ginger Solomon on *Calculated Risk*

"The *Gift of the Magpie* will leave you wanting more from this talented author."

~Kelly J. Goshorn on *Gift of the Magpie*

"*Calculated Risk* was one of those books I couldn't wait to get back to once I'd put it down…Loved it."

~Jan Elder on *Calculated Risk*

"I loved this story by Zoe McCarthy! The characters' dialogue zipped back and forth. It was fun and flirty with a message of faith and love."

~Sally Shupe on *Gift of the Magpie*

"I laughed with the characters and I felt their emotions along the way."

~Melissa Henderson on *Gift of the Magpie*

Dear Reader,

I remember times in my life when I felt invisible. My dad was in the Coast Guard, and our family moved often. For the first months at each new school, breaking into social circles was a tough job, some places harder than others. Although an introvert, I was willing to put myself out there, because I wanted friends. Maturity helped, but my true confidence came when I entered into a relationship with the Lord.

Possibly, you feel invisible at times in your life. If so, I hope God gives you the boldness and courage you need.

Blessings and joy,

Zoe

To my sisters in Christ in the Elk Creek Community Bible study.

Your love, support, and prayers are priceless. May God bless you with wisdom, truth, and peace.

Acknowledgements

Three people have been invaluable during the writing of *The Invisible Woman in a Red Dress.* As always, God revealed ideas and story problems to me when I quieted down for the night. My husband, John, read the story, shared his sticky-note suggestions, collaborated on the cover, and brainstormed ideas and rewordings. My editor, Denise Loock, carefully placed "awkward," "wordy," and "right word?" in just the right spots. Thank you, Lord, John, and Denise. I couldn't have completed the story without you.

"The thief comes only to steal and kill and destroy; I have come that they may have life, and have it to the full."

~ John 10:10

1

PASSION, DON, OR PAPUA NEW Guinea. Once again, Candace mulled the choices.

Don pulled his sedan into the no-parking space in front of her apartment building.

Always the same. All-you-can-eat pizza in noisy Luigi's and talking work with his friends, until they moved on to other subjects and she became invisible. Then ending up here in the apartment's no-parking space.

Every Saturday night.

Richmond offered movies, plays, and a historical canal walk. Even the state motto promised, "Virginia is for lovers."

Candace released her seatbelt and shifted to face Don. He cocked his ear toward a sports announcer's rehash of a basketball game on the radio.

"Kiss me, Don."

He glanced at her and held up a finger. "Just … one … minute." He leaned closer to the dashboard. Don already knew his team had won, yet not a face muscle twitched. His brown eyes remained focused on the radio knob.

Candace swung her knees away from Don, opened

the door, got out, and closed the door.

The car window whirred. Don bent over the passenger seat until he could see her. "Don't you want that kiss?"

"That's okay." She turned away and plodded up the snow-dusted sidewalk.

"Are you sure?"

She waved and kept walking. "I'll you see at work on Monday." She skirted a pink Big Wheel in the stairwell and shuffled up the cement stairs.

***

Inside her apartment, Candace dropped her handbag on the sofa and plopped down on a faux leather cushion.

Something had to change.

Her cell's retro-desk-phone ring jarred her. That ringtone was the first item she'd change. She straightened from her slouch.

Who'd call after eleven o'clock? Don? She slipped her phone from her handbag. Not Don.

Addison. Really? She was going to have to deal with her cousin right now?

Candace tapped the screen. "Hey. You okay?"

"Yes. I'm checking in. I want to know how you're doing." Addison, her substitute mother.

"I don't think you want to know." Candace held her cell to her ear with her shoulder and pulled off a boot.

"Of course I do. I'm your closest living relative."

"Actually, your mom's blood is more like mine than yours."

"Leave it to you to bring up a technicality."

"I'm sorry." Candace tugged off the second boot. "But I fear your calls. You always wrangle me into doing things I don't want to do."

"So, tell me how you are, then we both can get some sleep."

"Okay, but first I have a question. What are you passionate about?"

"That's easy. I adore my son, my husband, God, my church, my—"

"So you're a passionate person. You know what excites me?"

"What?"

"Nothing." Candace squeezed her eyes closed. "But I crave passion. I want to be crazy about a man, my job, helping people, my faith—at this point, about anything. I want children and a fierce love affair with my husband."

Silence.

She opened her eyes. Had she stumped her cousin? For once?

Addison let out a breath. "Wow. Where have you been hiding those feelings?"

"I've always wanted passion, but I don't know how to get it."

"Candace, it's simple. You have to put yourself out there before you can experience passion."

"What do you mean 'put myself out there'?"

"Look at it this way. You sit eight hours a day in front of a computer screen writing code, go out with the guy stationed in the cubical next to yours, and spend your dates with his friends—who are the programmer geeks who fill the other cubicles surrounding yours. You go to church and sneak out as soon as the worship service is over. You avoid passion."

"Are you stalking me?" Or had she spilled her guts to Addison before?

"I've compiled the few tidbits you've shared over the past two months. I'm concerned you aren't happy."

"I'm not."

"You don't want to be a programmer?"

"I like programming. And my work contributes to providing insurance for people, but with all the regulations and red tape, I don't feel like I'm helping anyone. Not even the company. On the rare occasions when I'm invited to meetings, I'm invited just to listen."

"Do you ever offer your opinion in meetings?"

"No one cares about the programmer's opinion."

Silence. Addison was probably biting her lip against repeating the bit about putting herself out there.

Addison let out a heavy breath. "Maybe you need a change."

"You're right. I need to figure out who I want to be and how to get there."

"You've said you have gobs of vacation days and can do your work from anywhere. Whenever you need a quiet place to think, your boss lets you work from home. Couldn't you take a few weeks off? Get away from work and Richmond to find your passion?"

Find her passion. Her new mantra. "But where could I go?"

A pop, like Addison smacking her lips, came across the line. "I know the perfect place."

"Well, spit it out, because I have no ideas."

"Go home."

The words hit her like a furnace blast. "I am not going to Grammy's house."

"It's been five years."

Candace's heart slumped. "It feels like yesterday."

"You need to go back, put the house in order, and sell it. Grammy rightly left it to you, but I cringe every time I picture the house closed up and rotting. It's the perfect place to sort out your life. Kill two problems with one heartache."

She'd rather go to Papua New Guinea and be a missionary than return to Grammy's house. And God knew for most of her adult life she'd been trying to buy Him off with donations to PNG missions. Anything to avoid the South Pacific trip.

"Are you there, Candace?"

"I'm not ready to deal with the memories, the house, and Grammy's stuff. Did you know she has a few hundred empty canning jars in the basement? I gave away half that many jars of snaps, bread and butter pickles, and tomatoes before I closed the house."

"Listen up, Cuz. This is the twentieth of January. I challenge you, Candace Parks, to take vacation and remote working days and drive the four hours to Twisty Creek. I challenge you to stay there until Valentine's Day. That'll give you almost four weeks to list Grammy's house with a realtor and to find your passion."

2

CANDACE'S FIESTA SEDAN CRESTED THE last mountain between Richmond and Grammy's house. Wow. The majestic presence of the mountain ranges and the richness of the hilly valleys, even in winter, had definitely dimmed in her memory. The blue mountain ridges that encircled Twisty Creek's valley welcomed her home.

Large rolling hills still hid Grammy's house, but Candace passed the redbrick elementary school where she'd attended fifth and sixth grades. She eyed the long set of swings where she'd spent entire recess periods allowing the back and forth movement to comfort her after she lost Mama, Daddy, and Jules. Now the building sat abandoned in the late Sunday afternoon sunshine.

Several cars were parked at the minimart and gas station across from the post office. She smiled. Downtown Twisty Creek, where rush hour was stopping at a stop sign to let one truck pass by.

As she approached the road leading to Grammy's house, her stomach muscles clenched. Would the house still be the tallest among the brick and wood-framed homes on either side of the road that eventually curved into the foothills? A battalion of goose bumps marched the length of her arms.

And there it was. She slowed the Fiesta. The other houses looked the same with their fenced cow pastures and harvested cornfields behind them, but Grammy's front cedar bushes covered the porch and house up to the second floor windows. The exposed side needed a power wash and maybe a paint job. Grammy's overgrown back field looked like a single rotten tooth in the row of flat pastures and bush-hogged fields.

Grass and weeds sprouted from the gravel in the driveway, which Danny Walker mowed when he cut Grammy's half acre of yard during the grass-growing seasons. At least, she'd arranged for lawn service after the funeral.

But the rest? So much worse than she'd expected. Her name was most likely a bitter herb on local tongues.

She wheeled into Grammy's driveway. A dark blue SUV sat in Miss Mildred's driveway a holler to the right of Grammy's patchy gravel.

Did the SUV mean Miss Mildred had died and new neighbors had bought the house? She swallowed against the knot that tried to grow in her throat. What a fool she'd been not to keep in touch with Miss Mildred, especially since she'd spied her grandson, Trigg, and his high school sweetheart, Lauren, in a Richmond Kroger.

Of course, they hadn't recognized Ms. Invisible,

and she'd backed her buggy out of the soup section and rolled down a different aisle. Both looked as beautiful as they had the day they were crowned homecoming king and queen. She knew Trigg a hair better than Lauren. Growing up, he'd stayed with Miss Mildred lots of weekends.

Keys in hand, Candace got out of the car and stretched. She walked to the back of the car and unloaded the bags containing her personal and work laptops. Hitching the straps over her shoulders, she tramped to the house and sidled between the tall cedars to the porch. Even though the late afternoon sun shone, the darkness on the porch made it hard to see the keyhole.

Inside, the bag straps slid from her shoulders and down her arms. The laptops clunked against the entry rug covering the hardwood floor. She clamped her hand to her nose and gagged.

***

Candace tied off the last of three large plastic bags. Clearly, field mice had picnicked and thrift shopped in Grammy's house every spring and fall for the last five years. The stench of urine burned her nasal passages. Raising the windows a few inches helped, but she'd drive to Galax tomorrow and buy a shelf's worth of fabric deodorizer. That should help until she could rent a truck and exile all the upholstered furniture to the county dump.

The downstairs was worse than the upstairs—the part she'd toured anyway. Maybe tomorrow she'd have the guts to open the door to Grammy's bedroom. Down here, the mice had pulled stuffing from cushions and pillows and gnawed off the fringe on the afghans adorning the sofa and armchairs. Colorful mouse nests turned up in nooks, cabinets, and drawers—fortunately empty now.

A brown stain on the ceiling looked ominous.

Movement beyond the side living room window caught her attention. A man wrangled a large box from the dark blue SUV. When he straightened and powered down the hatch, Trigg Alderman's head appeared above the box.

She backed into the shadows. He wore jeans, and a plaid shirt collar peeked from his leather bomber jacket. A farm boy's build that Don could only dream about was something she'd spent too much time dreaming about in high school. Wisps of Trigg's dark hair blew straight up in the winter breeze. Her heart pounded like a multi-crop threshing machine.

Dumb heart. Thinking it'd spotted the first clue to where her passion lay. Not appropriate. Trigg was married to Lauren. But why was he, and maybe Lauren, in Twisty Creek now? Maybe Miss Mildred was alive, but ill.

Trigg climbed the porch steps, toed the front door open, and carried the box inside.

Wasn't it bad enough that Grammy memories drew

blood from her heart at every turn in the house, without exposing it to the crush she'd had on Trigg since the fifth grade?

***

Candace propped the screen door open with one of Grammy's weathered cookbooks and wrestled the large plastic trash can onto the back stoop.

In the neighboring yard, Trigg sat on the top step of his porch, showered in light from the floodlights under the eave. His laced hands covered the back of his bowed head.

That didn't look good. Was Miss Mildred in a bad way or did Trigg have marital problems?

This wasn't the time to say "hey" to the hunk from high school. Could she get back inside her house without Trigg spotting her? Candace made sure the can wouldn't tumble off the porch and crash on the ground, freed the screen door, and put a foot on the threshold to sneak inside. A force pressed down on her shoulders. Really? The pressure remained. This was the first time she'd experienced godly pressure in a long time. *Okay, Lord, I'll go.*

Wiping her now sweaty palms on her jeans, she hiked across the yard toward Trigg. She should have combed her hair and gathered it into a ponytail, changed her T-shirt, and washed the mouse scent from her hands. Even smarter, she should have put on her coat. It had to be in the thirties out here.

She stood in front of Trigg's lowered head. "Hey."

He jerked up his head. "Oh, hey." He stood, descended the stairs, and proffered his hand. His skin was cold, as if he'd been out here awhile. "Trigg Alderman. Did you recently buy the Parks place?"

"No, I already own it." Just as she'd forgotten the magnificence of the mountains, she'd failed to remember the beauty of Trigg's blue eyes.

"So, you're finally moving in?"

"No, I'm moving out. We went to the same high school. I'm Candace Parks."

"You—" His jaw slacked. He pointed at her and then her house. "Well, hello." He stuck out his hand again. She obliged him. "I think we played softball together in your grandma's field."

"Yeah." If playing softball meant being assigned to the outfield to dodge Trigg and his friends, who didn't trust her to catch line drives or fly balls or scoop up ground balls. Or maybe they just didn't see her.

He rested a foot on the bottom step. "Where do you live now?"

"Richmond."

His eyes lit up. "Me too."

Me? Didn't he mean we?

"What do you do there?" He rested his hand on the newel post.

"Programmer for a small insurance company."

"I'm a pharmacist. I live and work on the south side."

He can't give her
the proper care

Zoe M. McCarthy

"My apartment's in Henrico County." Another godly nudge came. Her heartbeat quickened. "Are you all right? Before I came over, you looked bothered."

"It's Gram. She's getting up in age, and I don't think she should live here alone. But she won't come and stay with me. Living in Richmond, I can't give her the proper care she needs here."

"She's that bad off?"

"Yes and no. She gets around okay. A little slow on the stairs. Doesn't hear well, especially when she doesn't wear her hearing aids."

"That doesn't sound too bad."

"True, but last month, she stood on a step stool to change the batteries in the wall clock and fell. Fortunately, she landed in an armchair and only sprained her wrist. But it could've been worse. She could've lain on the floor for hours, maybe days."

"That's worrisome, all right."

"Today, I installed a seat in her bathtub and a handle on the wall so she can take her baths easier."

So that's what he'd carried into the house. Huh. The guy truly cared about his grandmother. Her heart warmed.

He ran a hand through his dark hair. "After her fall, I finally talked her into giving up driving and sold her car for her. She has plenty of friends willing to do her shopping, but she won't go with them."

"She doesn't go out at all?"

"No. She stays home and bakes them bread, pies,

13

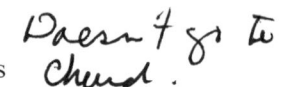

and cakes for their help. She doesn't go to church anymore, even when I'm here to take her."

"That doesn't sound like the Miss Mildred I remember."

"I know. My parents are divorced and my dad, her son, lives in California and travels a lot. I'm not sure what I should—" He clamped his mouth shut and wagged his head. "Was I chasing a dog down Sorry Lane, or what?" He gave her a droll grin. "Welcome back to Twisty Creek, Candace."

"No. That's okay. I'm glad you told me. I'll be here for four weeks. I'd be glad to shop for Miss Mildred and check on her a few times a day. Give you time to figure things out. As soon as I get the Internet hooked up and a temporary U.S. Cellular phone that picks up service here, I can text or email you a daily report."

His eyes widened. "Really? You'd do that?"

"It'll be no problem at all."

"That would help a lot. But I don't want to put you out. Things probably aren't as bad as I made out."

"You won't put me out. I'll be around the house most of the time. I plan to fix it up and put it on the market. And after this vacation week, I'll do my programing work from Grammy's house for another three weeks."

"That would give me time to research what kind of help is available." His face brightened as if an idea had taken hold. "And I can give you a hand with work on your house. During my high school summers, I worked in construction, and I've done all the repairs on Gram's house."

"I'll take you up on that. A nasty stain on the living room ceiling suggests a leak of some sort."

"I'll look into that. I'm on vacation this week too, but I come here most weekends. I work long days four days a week, so the three-day weekend helps ease the commute." He climbed a step. "Come on in and say hi to Gram."

She followed him into Miss M's house.

Not one mention of Lauren. Strange.

Stay put, heart.

***

Candace trailed Trigg through the mudroom to the kitchen.

"See if you can guess who this is, Gram." He stepped aside.

Miss Mildred looked up from stirring a delicious-smelling concoction on the gas stove. Beef stew?

Miss M laid the wooden spoon on the stove cradle and turned with arms opened wide. "Well, Candace, look at you all grown up."

Candace's eyes misted as she entered Miss M's embrace. Why hadn't she kept in touch? She wrapped her arms around the woman's girth and hugged hard, then pulled away. "I should have written you, Miss Mildred. I'm sorry I didn't."

"I understand, honey. You was grieving hard when

you left." Miss M held her hands. "I'm tickled you're here now. You'll have dinner with us."

Behind Candace, Trigg cleared his throat. "Remember, I'm meeting Wayne at the Mexican restaurant in Independence tonight." He checked his fancy watch. "In fact, I need to leave now."

"Candace will keep me company, won't you, honey?"

She sure would, even if beef stew wasn't bubbling on the stove. She nodded.

"You ladies enjoy your evening, but save a bowl of stew for me."

Could the guy have a more engaging smile? A ten-minute reunion, and her puppy love came back and nipped her heart.

Miss M cocked a look at Trigg. "Maybe."

He raised a hand and left. As Miss M opened a cupboard and extracted two bowls, the front door closed.

"Will you pour us some sweet tea, dear? The pitcher's in the fridge."

Candace poured tea into two tumblers. Miss M looked about the same. Maybe a little heavier, and her face wore an added wrinkle or two. "You haven't changed much, Miss Mildred. You must be eating right."

Miss M ladled stew into the bowls, more in one than the other. "I'm doing real good." She set the steaming bowls and spoons on the oak kitchen table.

"Course, if you ask Trigg, I've got one foot in my grave. Sit, honey." She gestured toward the chair where the fuller bowl lay, then sat next to her at the round table.

Once seated, Miss M offered her hand. Candace gripped her warm fingers, and Miss M thanked the Lord for the food and bringing Candace home.

The stew meat melted in Candace's mouth. The beef, carrots, onions, and potatoes, the biscuits, and the sweet tea sure beat a package of cheese crackers, a single-sized bag of kettle corn, and a soda—her normal fare in the evenings.

She had to know. "Does Lauren come with Trigg on most weekends?"

"Oh, honey, he's not seeing that girl anymore."

Candace swallowed a potato chunk, whole. She struck her chest with her fist as the morsel made its way down her throat. "I thought they were married." The words came out in a rasp.

"Thank the Lord, they're not." Miss M regarded her. "You all right, honey?"

Candace nodded and gripped her spoon tighter to stop her hand from shaking. If only she were back in Grammy's fetid house to contemplate how this news fit into her find-her-passion quest.

Miss M sipped her sweet tea. "I'm so glad you're here, Candace. Between you and me, Trigg isn't missing this flavorful stew because he particularly likes Wayne or Mexican food. Wayne's the manager of the nursing home"— Miss M's hand flew out to the side—"up yonder." She dabbed her lips with her napkin as if to hide how pursed they'd become from the insinuation she'd shared.

Was Trigg crazy? Miss M was no more ready to enter a nursing home than she was. Maybe the most popular guy in school that she'd drooled over up until a minute ago wasn't worth the spit. Then again, Miss M could've read Trigg's motives wrong. But right now, Candace had a different problem to address.

She spoke as gently as she knew how. "I'm here to get Grammy's house ready to sell. But I'll be here until Valentine's Day, so I hope you'll let me see a lot of you during that time."

Miss M's shoulders slumped a half-inch, but she patted Candace's hand. "You're always welcome here—any day, anytime."

They ate in silence, both probably composing a speech to deliver to Trigg.

Miss M dipped her biscuit into the stew gravy. "I sure miss your grandma. A day didn't go by that Thelma and me didn't have a conversation. And when you came along, as quiet as a field mouse, she wasn't the only one who felt like she'd gained a daughter."

Daughter? How could she have ignored this chance at motherly love for five years? Tingles traveled from the crown of Candace's head to her shoulders.

3

A LOUD DING-DONG STARTLED Candace as she threw sheets over the wood furniture in the living room. Well, the doorbell worked. Her first day in Twisty Creek and she already had visitors?

She left an end table half covered and answered the door.

Trigg stood on the porch darkened by the tall cedars, his hands in his back pockets. "Hey. I've come to look at the stained ceiling. Is this a good time?"

She opened the door wider, and he walked inside.

"Pee-yew!" How'd you survive the night in this stench?"

"The smell's not as bad upstairs. I'm going to Lowe's after lunch to buy cleaning agents."

"I'll go with you, but first let me check to see what supplies are needed. I'll also search the house for possible mouse entry spots. We'll get sealing foam at Lowe's too."

Comforting to hear the "we" after hours in bed last night worrying how to transform her neglected house into a home someone would want to buy. Her blood pressure dropped ten digits.

She pointed at the stain the size of her personal

laptop. "It's right there. I hope it's not the toilet leaking in the upstairs bathroom. I turned on the water to the house, but I haven't flushed that toilet."

"You go on with what you're doing down here, and I'll go up and take a look." He surveyed the living room. "What *are* you doing?"

"Did you know that Grammy and Grandpa built this house in the early sixties?" Trigg shook his head. "Grandpa was a builder. They were the first people in Twisty Creek to use drywall in their construction. Grandpa built lots of the homes in Twisty Creek using the innovative replacement to plaster."

"Interesting."

"I plan to remove the wallpaper in here and paint the walls a neutral color."

"Can I help you cover the chairs?"

"No. Those are beyond fumigating. They'll go to the dump. The other furniture I'm donating to Goodwill, except Grammy's rocking chair."

"I'll call Brayden Cole and borrow his truck to haul off furniture."

With all his offers of help, her blood pressure might register normal by the end of the day. "I'll pay you or anyone else whatever it costs to get this place in shape."

He cocked his head and frowned. "You must've been away a long time. This is Twisty Creek, little neighbor. Here, everyone helps their neighbors."

But she was not a charity case, big neighbor. "Money's not an issue."

He raised an eyebrow. "But who we are is. You buy the materials. My friends and I will take care of the rest." He started for the stairs.

"Trigg."

He stopped and turned. "Yeah?"

"Since you're in such a helpful mood, do you or one of your friends own a chainsaw?"

"Sure do."

She scrunched her shoulders and made a you-may-not-like-this face. "Would you find someone to cut down the cedars in front?"

"Done." He winked at her, then climbed the stairs two at a time.

Who'd have thought the high school football star and homecoming king would cross the threshold of her house and work on her toilet?

If only his good mood would remain when she confronted him about nursing homes and Miss M.

She'd pick her time.

After a half hour, Trigg clunked down the stairs.

Candace stood on a step stool and pulled another section of the wisteria wallpaper. It split near the ceiling and ripped away in a small section. Wallpaper remover solution would go on the Lowe's list.

She dropped the partial strip to the oak floor and stepped off the stool. "What's the verdict?"

He propped his hand on an armchair, wrinkled his

nose, and jerked his hand off the cloth upholstery. "Man, this chair stinks."

She stifled a laugh.

He crossed his arms over his ribcage. "The ring seal on the toilet has leaked. The water seeped through to the subflooring. Were you planning to replace the tiles upstairs?"

"I probably should."

"Then you've gotten your wish about paying for services. I can remove the tile, replace rotted subflooring, and put in a new toilet ring, but you need to hire a tile professional. I can recommend one." He looked toward the ceiling. "The good news is I can patch the stain from this level."

"I appreciate your help, Trigg."

"No problem." He rubbed his hands together. "Now, I'm going to take care of the cedars. After I hack down those monsters, if you'd like to, we can have lunch in Galax and then go to Lowe's."

"Would Miss Mildred want to come with us?"

"We can ask, but she won't go."

Maybe just the two of them worked best. That way, she could draw out his intentions regarding a nursing home for Miss M. "But isn't she expecting you to have lunch with her at the house?"

"Not today." He strode to the door. "I told her at breakfast I hoped to take you to lunch in Galax on our way to Lowe's."

"Trigg! You can't buy my lunch."

He stopped and faced her, his expression earnest. "Your offer to check in on Gram next week lifts a load off my mind."

She took three steps closer to Trigg and punched her index finger toward Grammy's hideous paisley carpet. "I'm from around here, and helping my neighbor, Miss Mildred, is who I am. No payment required."

***

Candace ran her hand over the leather on the bucket seat in Trigg's SUV and surveyed the knobs and buttons on the dash. "Wow. Upscale." Her secondhand Fiesta worked, saved a lot of money, and fit easily into parking spaces. But it was the pits for hauling materials from Lowe's.

Trigg glanced at her. "When I'm here, I miss having a truck. I could have cut the downed cedars into logs and hauled them away. But I'll do that when Brayden comes over with his truck." He maneuvered another curve in the road that wound through hills and valleys and along creeks.

"I'm glad the cedars are down." Candace shifted her attention from sheep grazing on a hill to his handsome profile. "Can I ask you something about Miss Mildred?"

"Sure."

"Are you going to put her into a nursing home?"

He chuckled.

Wow. Not the response she expected. Could he be so flippant? "What could possibly be funny about forcing your grandmother to move into a nursing home when she doesn't want to go?"

"It's funny for a barnful of reasons. One." He held up a finger from the steering wheel. "I told her I was not sticking her in a nursing home or even trying to scare her into coming to live with me."

Candace opened her mouth to thank Trigg.

"Two." He raised another finger. "There's nothing wrong with her mind. She put together that my supper with Wayne last night was to talk about her. Only thing is we were talking insurance. I understand insurance coverage for drugs, but Wayne is up on all the coverage changes to medical policies. Saved me hours reading through Gram's supplemental and Medicare booklets."

"You should tell her that. She was worried."

"I will. Again."

"The only issue I observed in my short time with Miss Mildred was her need to get out of the house once in a while—go to church, buy groceries, visit with friends."

Candace could hear Addison. *Your advice for Miss Mildred is what I've been trying to make you understand.* She'd not share this conversation with her cousin.

Trigg looked at her. "That's easy to say but it's hard to convince Gram to get involved in social activities for her own good."

Candace squinted. A dead polecat lay in the road ahead. "Skunk."

His finger shot to the button that closed off the air from outside. No skunk odor drifted into the SUV.

"Why else did you think my nursing home question was humorous?"

"Gram has found an advocate she can trust."

"Who?"

He turned toward her and grinned, giving her a glimpse of his toothpaste-ad teeth. "You." He redirected his gaze to the road before he entered into the next curve. "And … I've got myself a sparring partner."

Her, a sparring partner?

"You're a quiet gal, but you stand up for yourself. 'I'm from around here, and helping my neighbor, Miss Mildred, is who I am. No payment required.'" He'd stuck his nose in the air and used a high-pitched tone. "I'll have to watch myself around you."

Her cell rang. She plucked it from her handbag. Don. She silenced the annoying ring. "Sorry. I need to change that ringtone."

"It does have a piercing jangle."

Her cell rang again. "I'd better take this." With any luck, Don's emergency was a work problem she could take care of in a sentence or two. "Hey."

"What's going on? I thought we were friends."

She'd thought they were girlfriend and boyfriend.

"What's up?"

"Did you know Saturday night that you weren't coming in today?"

"No."

"Greg says you called him at home Sunday morning and said you'd be working remotely until mid-February. Didn't you think you should call me?"

So, Don had noticed she was missing from work at—she looked at the dash clock—twelve-ten. "Sorry."

"Is that all you're going to say?"

"Yes." She glanced sideways. Trigg had his eyes trained on the road, but those perfectly formed ears were taking it all in—if he considered juicy conversation *what's up, no, sorry,* and *yes.*

"You've been acting strange lately, Candace." She remained silent. "Are you being like this now because someone else is with you, or are you being a pain in the you-know-what?"

"Both. Sorry."

"Is it a guy?"

"Yes."

"Are we over?"

Why would he say that after he'd just said he thought they were friends? Kissing friends. "Probably for the best."

"I agree." He hung up.

She slipped her cell into her handbag. Had she ended a good thing—well, a fair thing— and would regret her off-the-cuff decision? Would she miss

Saturday night all-you-can-eat pizza?

Trigg looked over at her. "Everything all right?"

She nodded. Her shoulders felt less tense, and she breathed easier. She should have broken off whatever it was she had with Don a long time ago. Even though he'd shown some interest now, Don didn't care that much about their relationship.

"You're awful quiet." Trigg lifted two fingers from the steering wheel as a truck passed them from the opposite direction.

She chuckled. "You did the two-finger wave."

"Yeah. I reckon I did."

"Once I moved to Richmond, it didn't take me long to stop two-finger waves."

"People comment to you about the habit?"

She nodded. "Embarrassing. I changed the way I say things too, but I'm proud of my Southwest Virginia twang. It's not going anywhere."

"Mine either. I give the two-finger wave in Richmond. I like surprising people. You never know when a wave will brighten someone's day or give a city person something odd to share at the supper table." He looked her way.

She smiled.

"You've got a good-looking smile. You should use it more often."

He shouldn't give her compliments. A girl could get her heart broken.

***

Trigg grabbed a shopping buggy as they entered Lowe's. Candace's stomach pressed against her waistband. She hadn't eaten slaw-topped barbecue, hush puppies, and soft-fried potato chips in a long time. Between eating Miss M's home-cooked meals and lunching with Trigg, she'd have to buy larger jeans by Valentine's Day. The walk around Lowe's would do her good.

Trigg steered the cart toward the indoor plants. "Let's start on the first aisle and work our way to the lumber department at the other end. That way, you can see if there's anything else you need."

He stopped the buggy. She took two steps, then rotated toward him. What was he up to?

He held up a forefinger. "Let's play a game."

"In Lowe's?"

"Let's pretend we're married and building our first house."

She curbed her jaw from dropping. He was worse than crazy.

He drew his eyebrows together. "You don't look like you're on board. It'll be fun." He pushed the buggy forward and came alongside her. "Here's the scene. We've drawn up house plans for a two-bedroom house with a great room, kitchen, two baths, and a laundry room. Now we're here to purchase what each room needs. And the house next door has mouse, ceiling, wallpaper, and tile problems we're also going to fix. My name is Felix and yours is Marge. Ready, Marge?"

Candace moved aside to let a woman and her buggy pass. "Can't we just buy what we need for the house next door?"

He gave her a withering look. "Now, Marge, don't be a party pooper. It's been a long time since we've had a day away from the kids."

"Kids?"

"Yes, a boy for me, and a girl for you."

"Don't you think we need three bedrooms, then?"

Trigg lifted open hands. "Now you've got the hang of it. A slow start, but that's okay." He directed the buggy to shelves of houseplants.

Was she going to end up embarrassed and wished she'd never shown Trigg the stain in her house?

He swept a hand toward the plants. "Don't you think we need a few houseplants? Keep the oxygen level up?"

"I'm okay with whichever ones you choose."

He dropped his head back against his shoulders. "Marge, Marge, Marge. You're the botanist. You're the one who should select our plants. But I'll be glad to get us started."

He lifted a two-foot rubber tree plant with fat leaves. "I think this will be perfect between the window and the fireplace in the great room."

She checked to see if anyone nearby was listening to this idiocy, but no one seemed to be paying any

29

attention to them. "You're not going to put that in the buggy, are you?"

"Naw. We'll pick it up later. Okay, it's your turn."

She stared at him, but he didn't budge. She heaved a sigh and walked over to a shelf of African violets. One's bunch of deep purple flowers covered its furry leaves. So beautiful. "I think this would look pretty on the kitchen window sill."

Trigg's smile broadened. "I think you're right." He lifted the flowerpot and put it in the cart's child seat.

Her eyes widened. "I thought we were just pretending."

His dark-lashed blue eyes softened. "I think the house next door needs this violet."

As she nodded, her lips tipped up. The African violet would be a welcome sight each morning when she entered the kitchen to make coffee.

Trigg wheeled the buggy to the flooring section. "We have carpet, tile, laminate, hardwood, and vinyl flooring. Gotta tell you, Marge, I dislike carpeting."

"Me too. I like hardwood floors everywhere except for the bathrooms and the mudroom. If the kitchen is open to the great room, then hardwood flooring there, but if it's closed off, tile would work—" Oh my. Where had all that come from?

Trigg stood with his arms crossed over his chest, as smug as a car salesman who'd just sold a Cadillac.

Heat crawled up her neck. She turned away from him and brushed her hand along a length of wood on the display. The heat waned and her heart calmed. "I like this Antique Java hardwood." He stood beside her. She wandered to the laminate display. "You know what might wow the great room?"

He followed her. "What?"

She raised her hands and spread them apart. "Install the hickory laminate on one wall."

He leaned away from her, studying her. "That's a great idea, Candace."

She walked along the displayed laminates. "You mean, Marge, don't you, Felix?" She kept her face averted. Couldn't have him witness her enjoying his compliment.

***

Trigg's SUV looked like an insect. Two-by-fours protruded from the windows and a drywall sheet projected from the back. Everything secured, they climbed into the car and headed for Twisty Creek.

The Lowe's build-a-house game rivaled any event in Richmond for a good time. They'd picked out tubs, sinks, faucets, kitchen appliances, and crown moldings. By the time they reached the lumber section, Trigg had her laughing aloud, an activity absent from her daily routine for too long.

They stopped at a fast-food drive-in and ordered sodas.

As she sipped her soda, she regarded Trigg. He tapped his fingers on the steering wheel to a bluegrass

She'd keep her distance.

Questions his motives for flirting

tune on the radio.

Why did he enjoy entertaining her? It would've been so easy for him to take her to Lowe's and find the needed materials for their projects in half the time.

What if he considered her a charity case? Ugh. Or maybe Miss M commanded him to show her a good time so she'd stay indefinitely in Twisty Creek. Or perhaps Trigg thought amusing her for an afternoon was a way to repay her for checking on Miss M for the next four weeks. Her barbecue lunch churned in her stomach.

One day spent with him, and she had it bad for the man. The African violet and his two-finger wave captured her heart. She didn't even know if Trigg was dating someone in Richmond. Her trip home was supposed to be about finding her passion, not falling for an unavailable guy, or one beyond her reach.

From now on, she'd keep her distance, physically and emotionally.

Trigg lowered the volume on the radio. "Come with me tomorrow night and meet the old gang. They bowl every Tuesday evening."

"I never paid membership dues to the 'old gang.' They'd have no idea who I am."

"Sure they would."

"How? The only extracurricular activity I participated in was the geology club. I don't remember any of your gang being one of its six members."

"You might be surprised how many remember

They won't remember her
avoids
— bowling

you."

"I'd be shocked."

"Believe me, they'll remember you. I did."

Yeah, after she told him who she was. "Thanks, but I'll pass."

"It'd be neighborly of you to meet Brayden Cole. I'm borrowing his truck to take the furniture to the dump."

"I can't believe you're trying to make me feel guilty for not bowling, a sport I've tried once in my life."

"How about going just because I asked you to go?" He lifted his soda from the cup holder. "These days I'm on the outskirts of things here. I'd like you to accompany me as my friend from Richmond. You know, impress these Twisty Creek folk with our citified panache."

She laughed. "That was so lame. Okay. I'll go and dazzle them with my famous gutter-ball roll." Heaven help her, she had no resolve when it came to Trigg Alderman. Let the social disasters begin.

No self confidence

4

CANDACE STOOD AT THE LIVING room window, watching for Trigg to exit Miss M's house. She'd hurry out and meet him at his SUV. No way would she give him time to come to her door. This outing would not smack of a date.

No sign of him. She rotated and surveyed the living room. The raw walls already looked better than the wisteria wallpaper that had peeled off the wall at the corners and baseboards. The build-a-house game had seemed real this afternoon with Trigg upstairs prying the old tiles from the bathroom floor while she stripped wallpaper downstairs.

She turned and searched for Trigg. He closed Miss M's storm door. She grabbed her handbag and left the house. The downed cedars opened a shortcut, and the light from her porch lamps lit much of her yard, helping her speed walk to Trigg's car.

"The temperature must have dropped ten degrees since this afternoon," she called as she approached.

Trigg's head swung toward her. "I'd have driven over and rung your doorbell. No need for you to freeze your toes."

"No need for you to ring my doorbell."

He opened the passenger door. "Are we sparring?"

She slid onto the leather seat. "Only if you treat me like someone more special than a Richmond buddy."

"Oh ho! Touché. I'd better sharpen my épée."

"Uh huh."

He closed her door, skirted the hood, and climbed in. "Nervous?"

"Why would I be?"

"Meeting up with the old gang?"

Terrified. "Nope." She reached to brush her mane of hair off her shoulder. It wasn't there. Oh, yeah. She was so scared she'd forgotten she'd banded her hair into a ponytail.

He put the car in reverse. "You look pretty."

She couldn't win. The whole purpose of the casual ponytail and jeans was to discourage date talk from Trigg and his friends. Or maybe she was in denial about her motives. Weren't the breath mint under her tongue, the hint of lipstick, and the mascara a contradiction?

"Thanks. I wanted to make sure you lose the bet that your friends will recognize me."

"We had a bet?"

She rolled her eyes. "The altercation, or whatever it was."

"So you're saying you never put on makeup in high school?"

"Too busy looking for geodes to impress members of the geology club."

"Ha! I saw your smile. The dash lights are too bright for you to hide in the shadows, Marge."

She turned her head toward the window before he caught her smiling. She held up a hand. "Truce."

"No way."

***

Trigg beat her to the bowling alley door and opened it for her. Forget sparring. This was war. Funny thing was Candace had wished Don would act like a gentleman on their dates, and here she was discouraging Trigg. Truthfully, she liked Trigg's attention. But this was not a date, and besides, in these parts, manners were hammered into males from birth. She didn't rank as someone more special than any other woman.

As soon as the door whooshed open, whirring balls, the thunder of strikes, and bowlers' cheers begged her heart to step up to the excitement. She'd been ten years old the first and last time she'd entered a bowling alley. The energy of the place hadn't changed.

Trigg touched her arm. "What size shoe do you wear?"

"Seven." Candace followed him to the shoe counter.

"Candace."

She spun toward the voice. Brayden Cole stood with his hand outstretched.

"Remember me?"

Of course she did. Algebra One, freshman year.

36

Chemistry, sophomore year. French Three, junior year. U.S. Government, senior year. Cute and friendly.

She shook his hand. "Sure. Brayden, right?"

"You're Thelma and Arthur Park's granddaughter. Lived on Shadow Road with your grandmother."

Wow. Brayden did remember her. Amazing.

Trigg joined them carrying two sets of bowling shoes. "I see Brayden's introduced himself."

"More like getting reacquainted." Brayden led the way to the lanes.

Trigg walked beside her. "Did Brayden remember you?"

"Consider me shocked."

"See, I told you they would." His lips spread into a smug smile.

"One, so far. He was in one of my classes every year."

"I was in sophomore English with you."

"Actually, you were in Algebra One with Brayden and me in our freshman year."

"Not sophomore English?"

"Nope."

"That doesn't mean anything. Who can remember who was in every class in four years of high school?"

Yeah, she was a weirdo, all right.

They reached the lane, where Billie Jean Cox laced up her bowling shoes, and Grayson Grant dug his blue ball out of his bowling bag. Jason Saunders searched among the black balls stored behind the lanes. Sandy

Lee sat geared up scrolling through her cell. Had she and Jason married?

Trigg handed Candace the size seven shoes. His had elevens engraved on their backs. "You all remember Candace Parks." Everyone turned to her. Nods and greetings followed.

Candace sat next to Meg-Ryan-lookalike Sandy and kicked off her loafers.

"You've been gone awhile." Sandy tossed her phone into her handbag. "I heard you'd moved to Richmond. Didn't you live with your grandma next to Trigg's grandma?"

"Yes. Did you and Jason get married?"

"We've been married seven years. We have two little girls. Shelby's five and Sissy is almost three."

"Fun ages. As a teenager, I babysat a lot and enjoyed kids between ages two and six. Who do your children look like?"

"With their red hair, Jason, for sure."

Billie Jean sat on her other side. "Hey. Do you remember me?"

"Sure. You were in my English class all four years."

"Yeah." Billie Jean looked impressed. She also looked like she'd used a shoehorn to squeeze into her jeans. On the other hand, her dark hair was wild and free. "You lived in the house next to Trigg's grandmother. So, you live in Richmond now?"

Candace nodded.

"How do you like living in the big city?" Billie

Jean's gaze was locked on Trigg.

"I like the historical city, but the whole area is way too busy."

"Hmm."

If Billie Jean were given a test on this conversation, she would flunk. But at least everyone seemed to remember her. They connected her to Grammy and knew she'd lived next door to Trigg's grandma.

"I'd better find a ball." Candace left the lane area and tried out the bowling balls marked ten pounds. She found one that fit her thumb.

Grayson, a tall string bean, entered their names into the console, and the names showed up on the overhead screen. Ugh. She was up first.

Trigg, sitting in the chair beside Grayson at the console, pointed to a lane. "You're on that lane."

"I've bowled once in my life when I was ten. This is not going to be pretty."

"You may surprise yourself."

He'd been right about everyone remembering who she was, so maybe he'd be right about bowling.

Her first ball stayed on the lane, wandered to the right, and knocked a pin off the end. She turned to walk to the ball return. All eyes were on her, except Billie Jean's, which were on Trigg. Under such scrutiny, the skin across the back of her shoulders crawled as if she'd shudder at any moment.

"You can knock the rest down," Trigg said.

"Yeah, you still have a good chance for a spare."

From Brayden.

Hopefully, they wouldn't call for a vote, because the rest of the gang looked doubtful. If she could keep from twisting her hand, maybe she could upset a few more pins.

The ball didn't drift as far right the second time, and four pins dropped. A score of five was better than zero, right?

At the end of the first game, Trigg brought her a soda. She downed half the burning liquid. Who knew bowling was such work? Especially when six sets of eyes stared at her after each of her pathetic rolls. She'd finished with a forty-two, one less than the five-year-old on the lane next to their two lanes. The guys were good, except Jason, but he'd gotten a few spares and a strike. Billie Jean out-shone the other girls.

During the second game, Candace listened to the banter and laughter. No one said much to her, except Trigg and Brayden, which was fine. Billie Jean positioned herself next to Trigg at every opportunity. Trigg was kind to her, but the woman needed to wise up and play hard to get. Since when had Candace felt this bad and embarrassed for anyone, especially a rival?

In the third game, Candace beat her other final scores, knocking down seven pins on her ninth turn. Waiting for her last time on the alley, she sat beside lanky Grayson on the bench. Should she say something? Make Addison proud and put herself out there?

"You're a good bowler, Grayson."

"Thanks. I love the game."

"You dated Wanda Dean back in high school, right?"

His grey eyes brightened. "We got married and have an eight-year-old son, Grayson. We call him Junior."

"Does he bowl?"

"I'm teaching him. I just wish Wanda was interested in bowling." He sipped his cola. "You lived next door to Mildred and Arthur Alderman. I think you were in the geology club. I'd have liked that. I collect interesting rocks when I hike in the mountains."

The blood emptied from Candace's face. They all had a script that Trigg had provided them. None of them remembered her.

Grayson rose and lifted his ball from the return. She needed to get out of there. Now. To the restroom.

"You're up, Candace." Trigg's smile faded.

She must look like a ghost. She jumped up, grabbed her ball, charged to the line, and released the ball. Who cared where it went. The best direction would be toward Trigg's head.

The pins blasted in every direction. She rotated and approached Trigg, her eyes averted from the jerk. "I'm going to the restroom. I'll meet you at the car."

Claps and kudos followed her as she barreled toward the restroom.

***

Candace had barely begun to shiver before Trigg exited the bowling alley and strode toward his car.

He raised his hands as he walked. "What's the matter?"

"Unlock the door." The door lock clinked. She yanked the door open and climbed in.

Trigg folded himself in behind the wheel. "What happened in there?"

She shifted to face him. "I have never been treated so cruelly."

Trigg's brow wrinkled. "How?"

"You should be ashamed of yourself. What you did was unforgivable."

"What'd I do?"

"You gave them all a script—a pitiful script."

He leaned against his door and stared at her. "How do you know that?"

She jutted her head toward him. "Because, Trigg, they all had the same limited information you gave them, which shows you don't remember me in high school, either. And, Trigg, there was no geology club."

His eyes widened and his gaze moved away from her like he was searching for a way out of his blocked corner. His gaze shifted back to her. "Then why'd you say you belonged to the geology club?"

"Oh no. You're not turning this one back on me. I was just being playful. I never dreamed you'd believe there was a geology club. But imagine how embarrassed you'd be if you knew you were invisible, but then were pleasantly surprised that you were wrong. Then you find out everyone was patronizing you. You were still the man who in their minds never existed. The close-knit gang had one over on you. Manipulated you. How would you feel, Trigg?"

He opened his mouth to speak.

"You masterminded the ruse that makes me feel worse than knowing I was invisible in high school. Unnoticed, I can handle. But now I feel conspicuous as if there's a big green button on my forehead that says, 'Push for a Laugh.'"

He grasped the hand she'd been brandishing. She yanked it out of his grip. He reached forward, and she jerked both hands away until they thumped the passenger window. He snagged one and held on.

"Let me go."

"Candace, calm down and listen to me."

She went limp. No way could she exit the car and walk over twenty miles home in the dark. He was determined to have his say, and he was stronger than she was. So let him spill his empty words. But she didn't have to look at him. She turned her head toward the window.

Trigg ran his thumb over the back of her hand. "You're right, it was a dumb idea. But I never meant to hurt you. Far from it. I thought you could use some friends. I wanted to—"

"Befriend the orphan." She swung her head to face

him. "Did you ever consider I don't need or want friends here? I have a full schedule at the house. And I have plenty of savings to hire the people I need to help me. If I want friendship, I'm sure Miss Mildred will oblige."

He leaned toward her. "You have the most interesting eyes. They're like the stone in a mood ring. Right now, in the light of the street lamp above us they look as purple as your new African violets."

She stared at him. What did the color of her eyes have to do with their argument? "Is this another ploy to derail my anger? Well, it's not going to—"

He pressed his lips against hers, then pulled away.

Not a word entered her head.

"Did that derail you, so I can squeeze in that I'll never do anything so stupid again? That I'm sorry I made you feel degraded. That you're not invisible. That I promise I won't ever use the kissing tactic again to get your attention. That I couldn't think of another way. And, that I want to know if your passionate words just now were the most words you've ever said in one instance."

She held up a finger and closed her eyes, taking in heavy breaths through her nose. "I'm collecting my thoughts."

How could she collect thoughts that had scattered to places unknown? He'd kissed her. His lips had been soft and tender, full of "I'm sorry." Forget collecting. She'd have to create some new thoughts.

She spoke as calmly as she could. "You don't know me. At all. I'm not helping Miss Mildred for you. Whatever I do to help her, I'm doing because I want to help my friend."

A transparent wall dropped over his face. "Suppose Gram said she didn't want your help. How would you feel?"

He didn't wait for her answer. He started the SUV and drove out of the lot.

5

CANDACE AWOKE, AND HER EYES popped open. Trigg had kissed her. And she'd as good as told him to get lost.

She rose to a sitting position and slid her legs over the side of the bed. No way was she going to rehash the hurt, the kiss, and her harsh words this morning. She'd already spent hours mulling over and praying about them before she finally fell asleep, exhausted.

But something still nagged her, as it had while she prayed about forgiving Trigg and asking for his forgiveness.

She hopped off the bed and pulled the sheet and comforter to the headboard. What was it that kept chipping at her?

Passion.

What did passion have to do with last night?

Last evening's events rolled through her mind like a bowling ball headed for ten pins. Oh, goodness. How could she not have seen stars, as hard as the realization had hit?

Yesterday had been packed with passion—all connected to Trigg. Standing up to his unfair rule that she couldn't pay people to work for her, but he could pay her for helping Miss M.

And then, her slow start turning into full involvement in the Lowe's build-a-house game. How they'd squabbled over how to equip the master bath—a shower with two showerheads and jets versus a soaking tub.

She hugged a pillow and chuckled. They'd finally compromised, adding more square feet to the bathroom. He got his double shower with jets, and she got her soaking tub—with jets.

Then the anger she'd unleashed when he'd pulled his ruse with the help of his friends. Hmm. Passion better buried.

She fluffed the pillows and aligned them on top of the comforter.

The kiss teetered on the fence. Easier if it hadn't happened, yet something to cherish because it had. Humph. As if she had control of anything surrounding Trigg's kiss. She couldn't stop goose bumps from rising on her arms every time his soft lips came to mind, which was too often.

She tossed the throw pillows onto the bed. Right or wrong, Trigg stirred her feelings. Awakening her dormant passions, alone, merited her forgiveness. But could he forgive her?

She left the bedroom and stood facing Grammy's bedroom door. Was this the day she'd go inside? She reached for the knob.

The doorbell rang. Trigg? She scuttled to her room,

pulled on a sweater, and combed her hair. Her warm-up pants and wool socks would have to do.

In the living room, she opened the front door. No one stood on the porch. Had she dilly-dallied too long? But wait … a small box sat on the porch floorboards. She looked around. No sign of anyone.

She stared at the box. It couldn't be from Trigg. Last night, they hadn't spoken to each other on the way home. She'd thought he'd pull into his driveway and let her walk across the expanse between their houses. But the eternal gentleman, even when angry, had dropped her off at her front door.

She lifted the box and wiggled off the top. A foam square covered something underneath. With a finger, she raised the foam.

A mood ring.

She stifled a laugh with her hand. Where in the world did Trigg find a mood ring?

To protect her socks, she tiptoed down the steps and down the sidewalk between the felled cedars. She breathed in their fresh-cut scent, then continued to walk on the balls of her feet, until she could see Trigg's house behind hers.

Trigg and Brayden leaned against a shiny red truck. Trigg held a chainsaw and Brayden had a coiled rope looped over one arm.

Trigg raised the chainsaw. "Do we have permission to cut up your cedars, stack the logs in Brayden's truck, and haul them away?"

What was Trigg, and now Brayden, made of that they refused to give up on her? She hollered back, "Let me check my mood first." She slipped on the ring, which fit her right ring finger perfectly. She pretended to know what purple meant. "Please do."

The guys strode to her like ghostbusters ready to take care of a slimy apparition.

Trigg jerked his thumb toward the front door. "Better get inside before you freeze." He fired up his chainsaw.

She raised her hand bearing the mood ring, mouthed, "Thank you," and tiptoed into the house.

She inspected the mood stone. Still purple. Did purple mean passion?

***

Candace rolled Creamy Taupe Delight paint on the back wall, finishing the last section of the living room. Trigg and Brayden had hauled off the cedar logs and then loaded the truck with the upholstered settee, two arm chairs, and the rug. As they drove off to the dump, the truck looked like a camel. On a third trip, they'd taken the rest of the living room furniture to the Goodwill in Galax.

Now she backed to the front door and surveyed the room. The paint gave the place a fresh look. Maybe tomorrow she'd go to the furniture store in Independence and order furniture.

The doorbell rang. She laid her brush across the

paint can, hustled to the door, and opened it. Trigg.

He ran his forefinger across the tip of her nose. "Don't you look cute in a splash of paint."

She rubbed her nose on the shirtsleeve of her painting shirt, then stood aside. "Tada!"

"Wow. The room is coming along." He sniffed. "I don't smell the acrid mouse odor. And the house should stay that way. Yesterday, I sprayed foam around every pipe in the bathrooms and the kitchen."

"I've scrubbed the places I found nests, but I think getting rid of the furniture helped the most to eliminate the odor." She lifted her hand. "Thank you for the mood ring."

He peered at the stone. "It's purple. What does that mean?"

"I don't know."

"There was a folded chart under the foam stuffing in the box."

She retrieved the box from the kitchen. "Where'd you find the ring?"

"At Twisty Creek's favorite department store in Galax."

"You went there this morning?"

"It's open twenty-four-seven, and I got there at six."

She unfolded the paper. "Tell me you were there for something other than the mood ring."

"Well, I bought a doughnut." He stepped closer to her and peered over her shoulder. "So what does purple mean?"

Oh no. She whipped the paper down to face her thigh. Heat rose up her neck.

"You're too late. I saw the words. Sensual, excited, passionate, romantic."

"It also said tranquil, balanced inside, and satisfied." She swept her hand around the room. "I'm satisfied with how my new living room looks. The stone sensed that."

He snatched the paper from her hand. "You must love the room"—he grabbed her hand and raised it to expose the stone—"because the stone is turning a reddish purple. Which means—"

Candace swiped at the paper, but he held it out of her reach. He laughed as he looked up at the chart. "'Emotional state of passion.' The stone can't be wrong, Marge. You blushed just before the stone turned redder."

She frowned. Passion came up too often these days. Mostly at her expense. "Did you have ulterior motives in giving me this ring? It seems you're having more fun with it than I am." She snatched the paper from him and folded it. "By the way, where is Brayden? I wanted to thank him for all he piled into his truck."

"Uh oh." He smacked the heel of his hand against his forehead. "I was supposed to come get you for lunch. Hurry up. Gram's hamburger pie is waiting."

***

Candace and Trigg jogged to Miss M's. Inside, they

padded across the living room area rugs to the kitchen. Miss M's front room and furnishings mirrored the style and clutter of Grammy's house.

Brayden sat at the round oak table alone, sipping sweet tea. "What have you two been doing? I'm starving."

Trigg pulled out a chair for Candace. "Where's Grammy? I thought she'd be standing over the hamburger pie tapping her foot."

Miss M came in from the hallway. "There you two are. Sit. Sit. I had to get my hearing aids so's I don't miss the conversation. I couldn't catch a thing this"— she nodded toward Brayden—"mumbler said."

Brayden clamped his hand to his chest. "I don't mumble, Miss Mildred." He enunciated each word.

Miss Mildred swatted him with an oven mitt. "I'm on to you, young man. I know you stop mumbling as soon as I put in my hearing aids." She donned two mitts.

Had Miss M made a joke or did she believe her accusation? She turned and opened the oven, hiding her expression from the others. No one chanced a chuckle.

As Miss M drew out a casserole dish, a heavenly aroma snaked toward her guests. Three noses inched toward the oven.

"That smells wonderful, Miss Mildred." Candace sidestepped Miss M to close the oven door. "You used to make hamburger pie for Grammy and me on Friday nights."

"We're having it early this week. I thought with all the work you young'uns are doing, you could use a hardy lunch."

Miss M served up plates mounded with hamburger combined with a seasoned tomato sauce, quartered snaps, diced onions, and topped with a two-inch layer of mashed potatoes.

"That's the best aroma I've smelled in a long time." Brayden looked to Trigg. "Don't you tell Mom I said that."

Trigg chuckled. "Brayden's moved out but eats at least one meal a day with his parents."

"Hey. I bring them take-out pizza once a week."

Trigg rolled his eyes, then said the blessing.

Miss M fanned her napkin over her lap. "So, how's the house coming along, Candace?"

"You'll have to come over and see. No more cedars covering the house. You probably heard the chainsaw going."

"No, honey, I didn't. I don't hear too good these days." She turned to Trigg. "But that's no call to stick a body in a nursing home." She'd screwed up her eyes, then smiled.

Trigg raised defensive hands. "Far be it from me to stick you anywhere, Gram."

Had Miss M's joking meant Trigg had reassured her that he was not pursuing a nursing home option? Probably.

Brayden held up his plate for a second serving. Miss M obliged. "Candace, tell Miss Mildred what you're doing inside your house."

Candace set her tumbler on the red placemat. "I'm afraid you won't like how I took down Grammy's wallpaper in the living room and painted the walls a light taupe color."

"Honey, I watch that GHTV or whatever them letters are. I like to see young couples spiff up their dull houses. That's why you need to stay around here. Help me freshen my stale decor. I'm tired of this yellowed strawberry wallpaper in the kitchen."

Trigg stared at his grandma, then shifted his gaze to Candace and raised his eyebrows as if to say, "Who knew Gram was such a modern gal?"

Brayden nodded. "I'm with Miss M. You could start a business, Candace, doing do-overs for all the old houses around here. I'd hire you."

"For heaven's sake, y'all." Candace swished her fork. "I've painted one room in Grammy's house, and now I'm a decorator?"

Everyone chuckled, then returned to cleaning their plates.

Brayden stood. "I gotta go to work. Candace, if you need my truck or brawn for anything else, give me a holler." He pointed at Trigg. "Give her my number."

Miss M scooted her chair back. "You can't leave without a piece of my apple pie." She cut a huge slice from a deep dish, wrapped it with cellophane on a paper plate, and walked Brayden to the front door.

Candace laid her fork on her empty plate. "Where does Brayden work?"

"He works evenings at Lowe's—the one in Wytheville."

"I bet he'd be good at playing the build-a-house game."

Trigg grinned. "But nowhere near as fun a partner as you, Marge." He ran his fork over his plate and captured the last bit of mashed potatoes. "Gram sure loves to cook."

"Bring her over to see the house tonight. I'll make my one and only recipe from Grammy, pumpkin and black bean soup. Give Miss M a night off."

"Sounds good. Maybe Gram will leave the house and come, but I can't."

What did Trigg have planned for the evening that wasn't bowling, hanging out with Brayden, or involving Miss M?

***

Candace vacuumed the living room floor with Grammy's upright. The oak floors were in good shape. She would wash them with wood soap and then apply hardwood wax. But first, she'd satisfy her stomach growls.

Too bad Miss M begged off coming over. Candace had offered valet services from driveway to driveway, but Miss M held firm. So, rather than cook for one, she ate a bologna sandwich and a slice of Miss M's apple pie.

Candace glanced up from her vacuuming to the side window. Miss M's porch light revealed a black pickup truck pulling up behind Trigg's SUV. She shut off the vacuum cleaner and overhead light, and crept to the window.

The driver opened the truck door, and the cab light revealed Billie Jean. Billie Jean and Trigg? Billie Jean dumped liquid from a mug onto the driveway, then closed the door.

Candace had been wrong. Billie Jean's attraction to Trigg wasn't one-sided.

Trigg emerged from the house, made his way to the truck, and climbed inside. Billie Jean backed the truck to the road.

Standing in the dark, Candace tried to imagine why Trigg was attracted to Billie Jean. Coming up blank, she shuffled away from the window. When her shin connected with wood, she turned and collapsed into Grammy's rocker, the only chair left in the living room. She couldn't see her hands, but, boy, were they shaking.

Trigg and tight-jeans Billie Jean were an item? Really? Was Trigg entertaining Billie Jean with the same activities he'd done with Candace? Or was it the other way around? Had Trigg played the build-a-house game with Billie Jean first? Had he told her that her eyes changed colors like a mood ring? Did Billie Jean have a mood ring in her jewelry box?

What color was her stone now?

Her arms held out in front of her, she shuffled in the dark to the wall plate and flipped the switch to the overhead light fixture. The mood stone had turned from purple to a darkish orange.

She strode to the kitchen, flipped the light switch, opened Grammy's everything drawer, and unfolded the color chart. Next to an orange dot, the words read, "Worry, aggression, or tenseness." So which was it? Humph. What did a mood stone know?

She slipped the ring off and set it on the windowsill. Let the stone report the feelings of window wood. It had turned orange only because it'd reacted to the temperature of her skin. She'd been hauling the upright back and forth, and her hand was sweaty and hot. She wasn't worried, aggressive, or tense.

Candace dropped her chin to her chest. How about all three?

She returned to the rocker. The back-and-forth motion soothed her roiling gut, but, boy, her heart ached.

"Lord, I thought we were on a roll with finding my passion for a man. Was I wrong that You'd provided the right one? I worried You might be reaching too high."

Or maybe Trigg never blipped on God's radar. Perhaps Billie Jean's unexpected entrance was a reminder that God wanted her to go to Papua New

Guinea. Once again, God confirmed that sending a third of her salary to support missionaries and Bible translators in the South Pacific islands hadn't changed His mind.

God knew He'd given her a penchant for numbers, logic, and programming. He knew she had trouble speaking English to Americans, much less communicating with foreigners halfway across the world. But her God used unlikely people for His purposes. Finding her passion to help people would probably depend on her obedience to traveling to a remote spot. A place where she wouldn't understand a word anyone said, and in her ineptness, she'd do everything wrong. Plus, online posts written about scarce toilets and limited electricity didn't encourage her.

Perhaps the time had come to stop living for herself. But she couldn't get past one big fact. Her resistance to catching the next plane to PNG hadn't grown completely from uncharitable self-centeredness. All the years since college at Tech, when she'd sought God's will on becoming a missionary to PNG, He'd never led her to pack her bags. So she'd kept helping Papuans through her monetary gifts. Waiting. Wondering. Fearing.

6

CANDACE SAT AT THE KITCHEN table nursing a cup of coffee, her pay-by-the-month cell lying next to her cereal bowl. She stared at the device. "Go ahead, buzz and earn your fees."

She sat back and let limp arms fall to her sides. Would the day demand another flurry of activity so she'd have no time to imagine Trigg in Billie Jean's arms?

His text yesterday had been short. He couldn't work on the ceiling until Friday. Here it was Friday at eight-thirty. Did the rising sun promise a TGIF day?

One thing was for sure. Today, like yesterday, she would not open Grammy's bedroom door. She required a day void of negative emotions for that. Maybe she should slip the mood ring back on, and when the stone turned happy pink, she'd go inside Grammy's room to smells and memories—or a severe bout of grief.

Her dream last night didn't help her mood, either. The Richmond police drove with sirens all the way to Twisty Creek and told her she had to be on a plane the next day for Papua New Guinea. If she refused, she'd never find her passion. During her tug-of-war decision, she'd awakened and praised God she didn't have to choose—yet.

A text notification bleeped. Her heart flipped. She leaned forward. Don.

When r u returning? Guys & me miss u.

Yeah. Missed her like they missed a flower vase on the table at Luigi's.

She thumbed buttons.

Feb 15 See u then.

The doorbell rang. Candace leapt from the chair and inspected her hair in the chrome toaster. She'd "put herself out there" this morning and used her curling iron. She'd hoped the coils would relax into curves before Trigg arrived, but they were still tight. Ugh.

Did she really want to compete with Billie Jean? In Candace's case, squeezing her behind into jeans two sizes too small would only create a bed-slat look. Plus, she owned no such jeans. But her thick blond hair, shiny and soft to the touch, rivaled Billy Jean's wild mane.

In the living room, Candace counted to five, then opened the door. Trigg stood on the porch, gripping two large tool caddies. He was dressed in the leather bomber jacket, jeans, work boots, and a shadow of whiskers.

Which mood stone color meant swooning?

"Ready to say goodbye to your stain?" He stepped inside and set the tool caddies on the floor. He straightened. "Whoa. The floors look fantastic." He scanned the room. "You got a lot done yesterday."

"Yeah."

Yesterday, she'd had a choice. Stress over Billie Jean getting her hooks into Trigg or occupy her mind and body with tough decisions and hard labor. So she'd shopped for curtains, ordered furniture, painted baseboards, and cleaned, waxed, and polished floorboards.

Trigg performed a slow rotation. He lifted the edge of a red curtain panel draped over the back of the rocker. "These will be an improvement over the frilly white curtains." He walked over to two long boxes by the fireplace. "Well, I'll be, Marge, you're going to construct an accent wall with laminate wood. How'd you get the boxes home?"

"They protruded from the passenger window. It was a cold drive home."

"I bet."

"I'm going to apply silicone adhesive caulk to the planks and attach them to the walls."

"You'll need a chop saw to cut the planks."

"I thought I could use this." She rifled through her purchases piled in the corner opposite Trigg's tools. She lifted a small saw.

"You're only staying four weeks, remember." He cocked an eyebrow at her. "I'll find a chop saw you can use."

Humph. She'd wanted to start on the wall while

Trigg fixed the stain—in case she needed help.

"Don't look all pouty-faced. I can have a chop saw here in fifteen minutes."

She smiled. "That'd be great."

On his way to the door, he pulled one of her curls, and it snapped back. "Your hair looks pretty, Marge."

***

Trigg kept his word. He returned with a chop saw he'd borrowed from the O'Gradys at the end of the road.

He plugged in the cord. "Come here."

She walked over and stood beside him, holding the safety glasses he'd given her. The operation of the saw looked straightforward, but obviously, she'd receive a lesson anyway.

He crossed his arms over his chest. "What's the first rule?"

It was going to be a long morning. "Switch on the saw."

"No. Measure twice, cut once."

"I know. I thought that was rule number five."

"Maybe I liked you better as invisible."

She punched his arm.

"Ow!"

"You deserved worse."

He chuckled. "You have to admit it was funny."

She turned her head away to control her traitorous lips.

He laughed and drew her chin toward him. "See, you think it's humorous too. There's hope for you yet, Marge."

"Just show me what buttons to push and get on with fixing my ceiling. Please."

He grasped her arm and pulled her between his well-developed chest and the saw. While he explained the workings of the chop saw, she could smell a hint of spicy sandalwood. Maybe he could smell her lemony shampoo.

His chin brushed her hair. "Got it?"

"Um. Would you go through that again?"

She sensed him staring at the top of her head. He sighed. "You put on the glasses, flip that, line up the plank here, and pull this down slowly."

"Got it."

When he moved to the fireplace, the warmth of his nearness dissipated. He opened one of the two long boxes, and slid out a plank. "To get you started, let's measure the wall."

"Twice."

He paused in laying the plank aside and pinned her with a wry look. "Yes, twice."

She handed him a yardstick from her pile of materials.

He regarded the stick, then arched an eyebrow her way. "What kind of DIY woman are you?"

He plodded to his pile of tools and grabbed a metal tape measure. "Are you thinking a horizontal or vertical lie?"

"Horizontal."

Trigg was right. Without him, building the laminate wall would probably take her weeks instead of days. She could get used to a guy who got involved in her projects. Especially a man who didn't take over the job. It'd been a long time since she'd enjoyed teamwork. Don's idea of teamwork meant he brought his programming problems to her and she fixed his code. Trigg seemed eager to teach her how to successfully complete her project.

Once Trigg had helped her install three planks, he set his ladder under the ceiling stain. He removed a section of the ceiling with a drywall saw. "You know, I do remember you."

She cut a plank—after she'd measured twice. "How?"

"You and Miss Thelma had dinner with Gram, Granddaddy, and me." His head disappeared partially inside the rectangular ceiling hole. "Gram told me to show you the card city I'd made in the room where I stayed when I spent weekends with my grandparents."

True. He'd constructed houses, stores, and churches from playing cards he'd glued together. The village covered the hardwood floor from the bed to the door.

He stepped down two steps and faced her. "No structural damage."

"That's good news." She cut another plank. "I was fascinated with the town you'd built."

"Could have fooled me. You walked around my village and nodded. Not a question or a comment." He descended the ladder.

Candace applied the caulk to the back of a cut plank. "A lot went on inside my head that never passed my lips."

"To me, you seemed unimpressed." He expanded the tape measure and marked a piece of wallboard. "I don't think you came again to a meal at Gram's house while I was there."

She stopped gluing. "I'm sorry, Trigg."

"Nothing to be sorry about."

"I didn't put myself out there back then."

"Right." He looked up and gave her a tender smile. "It's not entirely the fault of others that they don't remember you."

"Did I ever say it was?" But maybe she'd implied it. Was she that needy?

"No, you didn't." He grinned. "I'm glad I've discovered how to push your express-yourself button."

Oh, he pushed her buttons all right. Her passion-about-life button, her anger button, her infatuation button, and her jealousy button. Because he spent time with Billie Jean, she needed to protect herself from the reject button.

Candace moved her ladder closer to the wall and climbed several rungs. "Would you hand me the caulked board?" She took the plank he lifted, locked it with the board above it, and pressed it in place. With a rubber mallet, she tapped along the length of the laminate board until it appeared flush with its neighbor.

She descended the ladder, and they stood together viewing the partial laminate wall.

Trigg anchored his hands on his hips. "I like it."

She cocked her head one way, then the other. "Me too."

After he'd finished taping the new wallboard section into the ceiling hole and applying drywall compound, he washed his implements in the kitchen sink, then returned to the living room.

He pointed to his repair job. "After the drywall compound dries, you'll need to sand that smooth before painting." He glanced around the room. "What time is it?"

She slipped her cell from her pocket. "Eleven-fifty."

"I gotta go." He strode to his tool caddies. "I'm late. See you tomorrow." He grabbed his coat and left the house.

Candace abandoned the chop saw and speed-walked to the side window. Trigg jogged to Billie Jean's truck in his driveway and climbed inside.

***

Candace slumped into the rocker. How obvious did circumstances have to be? Trigg liked her—Candace. The girl next door. A friend. But he wanted to be with Billie Jean.

Clumping came from her porch outside, then the doorbell rang.

The visitor wasn't Trigg. He was gone. And Miss Mildred didn't wear boots that clomped. Maybe the person would go away if she stayed still. She needed to be alone to fully experience her misery.

The doorbell rang, and she jumped.

What kind of salesmen lived around here? Couldn't they take a hint? She plodded toward the door and opened it a crack. Brayden.

"Hey, Candace. Miss Mildred said you'd be home."

She swung the door wide. "Come in." But don't stay long.

Brayden surveyed the room. "The place looks good. I like what you're doing with that fireplace wall."

"Thanks." Now if he'd get to the point of his visit.

"What else are you planning to do in here?"

"Oh, a few things here and there."

He nodded.

Couldn't he leave? She had serious pouting to do.

Put yourself out there.

Addison was right. Brayden was kind enough to come visiting after he'd hauled trees away and trucked furniture to the dump. The least she could do was give him a few minutes of her sulking time. "Actually, I have new furniture ordered, and new window treatments to put up, and I want to paint the mantel. Then this room is done."

"Trigg said you're going to sell the place."

"Yes. I'm here until mid-February to get the house ready to put on the market."

He nodded.

Boy, her eyes would look stunning if she had the thick lashes that lined Brayden's gray eyes.

The silence became awkward.

"I understand you work at the Lowe's in Wytheville." She gestured toward him. "You're one of those guys I pelted with questions yesterday in the Galax Lowe's."

"Yeah, and I better skedaddle to work. I was wondering if you'd like to go to the Rook tournament tomorrow night. I'd pick you up around 6:45. It's at the firehouse. We have a big social room in the back."

"We?"

"I'm a volunteer fireman."

Impressive. Maybe spending time with Brayden would hoist her out of her funk and off the Trigg track. "I wouldn't have to play Rook, would I? I don't remember how to play that well."

"No. We provide hotdogs, chips, and sodas. Folks eat, play, and socialize. It's one of our biggest fundraisers."

Like most people in Twisty Creek, Grammy had played Rook and entered Rook tournaments. She'd taught the game to Candace. It was fun, but Candace hadn't played since she'd moved away. Most people in Richmond had never heard of the game. "I'd like to go."

His charming smile broadened. "Well, all right. I'll be by at 6:45."

Brayden left, and Candace closed the door.

Trigg wouldn't be the only one picked up in a truck.

7

BRAYDEN USHERED CANDACE INTO THE firehouse's large back room. People packed the place. Over their loud conversations and laughter, an announcer on a bullhorn assigned partners to twenty or so tables of four players each. Brayden grasped her hand and forged a path through the crowd whose male-to-female ratio was about fifty-fifty. Even a few teens peppered the throng.

Over all the commotion, Brayden must have heard his and his partner's names called. He seemed to know where he was headed. Avoiding feet and elbows, she hadn't paid attention to the announcer.

Brayden worked his way to the corner of the room, stopped at table sixteen, removed his cowboy hat, and placed it on an empty chair. He introduced Candace to the gray-haired husband-and-wife team sitting across from each other at the table. She smiled and shook their hands. Gentleman Brayden stood beside Candace while he waited for his partner.

Brayden's minty breath tickled her ear while he explained how the tournament worked. Like Trigg, his jeans hung just right on his hips and his boots were scuffed. His long-sleeved plaid shirt covered broad shoulders. He'd released her hand when they arrived at the table, but hers remembered his warm, and slightly rough fingers. He was all cowboy.

"This is a double-elimination tournament." He stood closer, his woodsy cologne scenting the air. "That means losers still have a chance to win. Final winners get their names on the plaque at the front of the room."

Candace nodded. Maybe Brayden could fill the passion-for-a-man opening on her passion chart. Perhaps God did have a man for her on His list—just not Trigg. She'd remain open to the possibility.

Billie Jean emerged from the crowd, Trigg in tow. They were not holding hands.

Billie Jean waved. "Hi, Candace. Brayden. I'm over on the other side at table twelve. See you guys later." She tootled her fingers at the couple sitting at the table. "Hey, Mr. and Mrs. Tanner."

So Billie Jean's partner was not Tr— Wow. Speaking of cowboy. Trigg had a notch up on Brayden as he stood with his cowboy hat in his hand. The city-dwelling pharmacist in his blue oxford shirt and khaki slacks had morphed into a cowboy. From his slick-backed dark waves to his cowboy boots, he rivaled a younger version of Timothy Olyphant of *Justified* TV fame. All he needed was a cheroot caught between his teeth for a rough, tough cowboy look.

Brayden slid back his chair, transferred his hat to the floor under the seat, and sat. Candace stood behind her cowboy for the evening.

Trigg's raised eyebrows suggested he'd been surprised at her presence. But he was no more surprised than she was when he sat in the chair opposite Brayden's. But of course Trigg would partner with Brayden. They'd been good friends ever since she could remember.

Who'd have known that her toes, which refused to curl in response to Don's sandals buckled over wool socks, would coil now over two handsome, boot-wearing cowboys? Where was a fan when a body needed a cooling breeze?

Candace stuffed the laugh bubbling inside her throat. This evening promised a good time for the city-dwelling lady dressed conservatively in a collared white shirt, blue V-neck sweater, correct-sized jeans, and black ankle boots.

As Candace watched Brayden play his cards, the rules and strategies of the game came back to her. Trigg and Brayden played well as partners and won the first round against Mr. and Mrs. Tanner. The cowboys' finesse may not have been the sole factor in their win. Mr. Tanner bid his cards too conservatively. Then again, innocent-eyed grandma, Mrs. Tanner, stretched every hand to the limit.

Surprisingly, one thing hadn't hurt their game. Candace had glanced up from Brayden's cards several times and caught Trigg staring at her. What did Trigg's attention mean, especially with Billie Jean in the equation? Maybe he couldn't believe the invisible woman had put herself out there with his buddy.

While the announcer re-paired the teams, Brayden left Candace standing with Trigg and threaded his way to the food tables.

Trigg elbowed her. "Why aren't you playing?"

"Haven't played in years. But after watching you guys, it's all coming back."

Would he ask her whether she was alone or had come as Brayden's date? But she and Brayden together hardly counted as a date. They were two friends who decided to come to the same event—never mind that Brayden picked her up, held her hand through the crowd, and was now getting and paying for her hotdog, chips, and a soda. Just friends.

"We'll have to play next weekend when I come back." He grinned. "I'd like to see how aggressive you are."

"Why?"

"I find you an interesting study."

Really? "You mean like a lab mouse?" Maybe he could study her boot in his shin.

"Oh, you're no mouse. There's a spark or shine that lies beneath your surface that piques my curiosity."

Oh, okay. She was good with having a spark or a shine. "You're on. Rook next weekend."

She'd show Mr. Cowboy how aggressive she could become when it came to winning. Addison refused to play games with her anymore, from gin rummy to

Monopoly. Of course, Don preferred to watch TV. No chance to show her aggression there. She'd even let him control her remote. Humph. Man, she never realized she'd allowed herself to be so passive.

Brayden arrived laden with food and two capped sodas in a cardboard drink carrier. "I hope you like mustard on your dog."

"Is there any other way to eat a hotdog?" She relieved him of half his load, and they followed Trigg to table ten.

Her soda went down well for a woman who'd earlier needed a fan. Brayden polished off his hotdog in four bites and sat across from Trigg. He and his partner had a game to win.

Billie Jean sailed by and ran her hand over Trigg's shoulders. "Don't you boys get too confident. Sandy and I won our match and plan to keep on winning."

"I'm sure you will … except the last match," Trigg called after her. "My partner has a few cards up his sleeve." He winked at Brayden, who pointed to his chest and raised questioning eyebrows.

Billie Jean lifted her hand and kept walking.

Why did Candace's heart flatten like a punctured tire when Trigg and Billie Jean were together? She had a perfectly good cowboy sitting right in front her, who'd asked her out, smelled good, and knew a hotdog should be eaten with mustard.

***

Brayden and Trigg shook hands with their losing opponents and then gave each other a cowboy-like hug. They'd won the tournament. No surprise. She and Brayden had wandered over to the large winners plaque during the second paring. Brayden's and Trigg's names showed up often on the brass tags, sometimes together and sometimes with other partners. Billie Jean's did too, once with Brayden and once with Trigg.

Tonight, though, Billie Jean and Sandy lost in the round after Billie Jean had made her vow to keep winning. Once out of the running and after each pairing, Billie Jean pulled up a chair behind Trigg. She patted his shoulder when she thought he'd played the right card and cheered when he and Brayden won a match.

Trigg seemed to concentrate more on the game after Billie Jean arrived. Probably didn't want her to catch him studying Brayden's date.

Billie Jean acted a bit too hyper and overbearing for her own introverted style, but Billie Jean was friendly and had something—unknown to Candace—that Trigg considered endearing.

After Trigg and Brayden signed the winners form and well-wishers had finished patting them on the back, Brayden found Candace next to the winners plaque. "Ready to go?"

She nodded and entered the stream leaving the firehouse. Brayden placed a guiding hand on her back.

In the parking lot, Trigg stood with Billie Jean, Sandy, and Jason. Trigg conversed for a moment, turned, and sauntered toward his SUV as the others piled into a sedan.

Did Billie Jean's catching a ride with Sandy and Jason mean Trigg would drive straight home? Candace's stomach flip-flopped. How could she delay Brayden so they didn't pull up to her house at the same time Trigg turned into his driveway? She imagined Trigg going inside Miss M's house and heading for a front window to spy on his best friend and his date. Her face heated.

At Brayden's truck, he opened her door. Was this the time to sprain her ankle? Have a sudden need to go back inside to retrieve her lipstick from the ladies restroom? Throw up?

Trigg waved to them, then climbed into his SUV.

She looked up at Brayden. "Do you mind if I run back inside for a minute?"

Brayden was too polite to ask what she was up to.

She strode to the door and wormed her way inside through the departing crowd. In the restroom, she stood in a stall and counted to a hundred as toilets flushed, water ran, and paper towels were ripped from dispensers.

Once outside the restroom, she joined the people exiting the firehouse. Trigg had pulled his SUV up to Brayden's truck window and the two men rested their arms on window rims and chatted. Candace's heart sank. Doomed.

She crossed the lot to Brayden's still opened passenger door. The truck's heater roared to battle the cold. She climbed inside and shut the door.

Trigg raised a hand. "Catch you guys later." His SUV rumbled toward the exit.

Brayden regarded her in the light from the parking lot lamps. "You okay?"

"I'm fine."

He inserted his key in the ignition.

Stall! Think! She pointed toward the firehouse. He looked back.

"How often do you get called out?"

His fingers remained paused on the key. "Since I work weekday evenings, I'm on call during the mornings. So maybe one to three times a month."

"Do you drive the trucks?"

"Sometimes, but not usually." He cranked the engine.

Hopefully, either Brayden drove slower than Trigg or her questions had delayed their trip home long enough for Trigg to make it inside Miss M's house.

***

Brayden backed into Candace's driveway. "Backing in is the fireman in me." Brayden killed the engine.

"No problem."

No sign of Trigg's SUV next door. Had Trigg followed Billie Jean's group? But then why hadn't

Billie Jean ridden with Trigg?

Brayden faced her. "I hope you enjoyed yourself."

"I did."

"I'd like to see you again sometime when we can actually talk. Get to know you better."

She glanced toward the road. No headlights coming their way. "That'd be fun."

"Good."

Why did Brayden have to be a cool, handsome, kindhearted guy who was interested in her but lived in Twisty Creek, a place she'd be leaving after Valentine's Day? And why did Trigg have to live in Richmond where she resided, but chose to pursue a Twisty Creek girl? It made no cosmic sense.

Brayden ducked his head to look up at the sky. "We're supposed to get some snow tomorrow."

"I'd like one good snow before I leave. Richmond's snowfall is usually wimpy." She turned toward the door. "Thanks for supper and a fun evening."

He laughed. "Wow. A real elegant meal. Maybe I could take you to dinner next Saturday night."

"I'd like that." Her skin crawled. She should tell Brayden there was no use in them dating when it would never work. Stopping things now would be kind. They lived too far apart, and her idiotic heart couldn't stop thinking about unavailable Trigg.

Headlights beamed as a vehicle came around a curve.

She grabbed the door handle. "Well, thanks again.

I'll see you soon."

"Do you need some help this week on the house? I'd be glad to help with anything, even hanging curtains."

The headlights grew in size and intensity. She pulled down on the handle. "I'll let you know."

"Did Trigg give you my number?"

The vehicle coming their way slowed. She opened the door wide. "I'll get your number from Trigg tomorrow."

He slid his phone from his pocket. "Let me get yours."

Trigg's SUV pulled into his driveway. "I don't know it. Tuesday, I bought a U.S. Cellular phone that gets reception here. I'll call you tomorrow."

Before he could speak, she closed the door and hurried to the porch, up the steps, and into her house.

8

CANDACE CREATED A FEW WAVES with her curling iron and applied light makeup. Yesterday, Miss M had refused her invitation to drive her to church. Why didn't Miss M want to go out? Did she have that fear-of-leaving-the-house disorder? Candace would add this concern to her prayer list.

She pulled on her black pencil skirt and black knee boots.

Oh, yeah. Last night, Brayden had said snow was expected for Twisty Creek. Candace crossed the room to her bedroom window facing the back of the house. A two-inch-thick blanket of snow covered the fields, except hers. There, snow capped the tall grass and dead thistle. She would ask Trigg to suggest someone who could bush-hog that mess as soon as the weather improved. She might have to wait until spring. Probably few people would look at the house before then anyway.

But her field aside, the snow-covered landscape was beautiful. Except for the O'Grady's snowcapped red barn a few fields over, everything in her view was white—the mountain ranges, hills, and valleys.

Although Richmond had its beauty, it couldn't beat Twisty Creek's.

She finished dressing, collected her Bible, and left the house.

The short drive to the church didn't allow the Fiesta to heat up before Candace turned into the parking lot. Her dash broadcasted she was a minute late. She bustled to the front doors, stamped snow from her boots, and entered the narthex. A man who looked familiar, but whose name refused to come to mind, welcomed her and handed her a bulletin.

At the entrance to the sanctuary, she froze. Whoa. Where had all the people gone?

When she'd lived here, the church was full. Now, a third of the people who'd attended five years ago sprinkled the pews. If lamenting meant what she thought it did, her heart was lamenting big time.

Trigg sat alone about halfway to the altar rail. Why was she surprised he'd come? She could picture him accompanying Miss M, but not coming on his own.

The organist played the prelude. As Candace walked up the aisle, heads rotated toward her, recognition brightening the faces of people she remembered. She stopped at Trigg's pew. He looked up, then scooted over to make a place for her on the green cushion. He gave her a smile, then trained his attention on the altar area, where a grey-haired woman lit two candles.

She leaned toward him and whispered, "Where is

everybody?"

"Many of the old have died, and many of the young"—he touched his forefinger to his knee then to hers—"have moved away."

"Sad."

He nodded.

The service proceeded. Sitting next to Trigg felt comfortable. He held the hymnal for her and sang in a rich baritone. For the unfamiliar hymns, she followed Trigg's lead, raising and lowering her pitch a nanosecond behind his until she got the hang of the tune.

At the end of the service, people approached them. As Trigg stood nearby, talking to neighbors concerned about Miss M, Candace received hugs from Grammy's friends. Most asked whether she intended to move back, adding they hoped she would.

A vibrating sensation warmed her. The stirring came on as strong—no, stronger—than her sorrow over her dying home church.

Outside, Sarah and Jason joined Trigg and Candace.

Trigg shook hands with Jason. "Where are Shelby and Sissy?"

"They spent the weekend with the grandparents. We're meeting them in Independence for lunch and the exchange."

Although Trigg had moved from Twisty Creek before the girls' births, he knew and called them by their names. Knowing their names, alone, won him a gold-star sticker. If the choice was up to her, she'd found her passion for a man. The wrong man. Why had Trigg picked Billie Jean?

After Trigg and Candace said their goodbyes to Sandy and Jason, Trigg walked Candace to her car. "I'm leaving from here to return to Richmond."

According to her drooping heartstrings, she already missed him. "I'll check on Miss Mildred and keep you updated."

"I appreciate that." He reached for her door handle, then stopped. "I'm going to have lunch at the Chinese restaurant in Wytheville near the interstate. Why don't you follow me up there, and I'll take you to lunch?"

"I'd like that." Had she hopped on his invitation too quickly? "But you don't have to buy me lunch."

"Oh no. Not that stubborn streak again. You let Brayden buy you supper last night. Why can't you let me do the same?"

So, her date with Brayden hadn't evaporated from Trigg's memory. "Okay. You may buy me lunch."

He opened her car door. "Did you enjoy the tournament—of course you did. Your date and I won."

"Why are you so curious about my date?"

"Before I take you for spicy Schezwan pork, I was wondering if you were all right now."

"Why wouldn't I be?"

"Brayden and I talked awhile after you went inside last night. He said you had to hurry back inside the firehouse, and then when he brought you home, you rushed inside your house. He wondered if you'd had a bad reaction to the hotdog."

Heat hotter than Chinese red peppers raced up her neck and face.

***

The hostess at the Chinese restaurant sat Candace and Trigg in a corner booth.

Without opening his menu, Trigg slid it to the table's edge. "I appreciate you driving up here to keep me company."

"Thank you for lunch." And thankfully, he hadn't pressured her for more information about her escapes from Brayden's truck last night.

Candace perused her menu. "Do you eat here every Sunday?"

"Can't beat their all-you-can-eat Sunday buffet. Then, from here, only three and a half hours to Richmond."

She closed her menu and set it on top of his. "I'll have the buffet too."

Once they'd visited the spread of Chinese delights, their server brought Trigg's soda and her hot tea. Trigg asked for chopsticks, which the server supplied from her apron pocket.

Did Trigg think he could embarrass her a second time today? Let him try. She broke apart her chopsticks, positioned them between thumb and fingers, and aptly pinched a water chestnut. "What do you do in Richmond all week?"

"Remember, I work ten-hour days and travel here on Fridays. So I mostly work." He drew a business card from his yellow oxford shirt pocket. "Speaking of remembering." He slid the card across the table. "I called Randy Barnett, and he said he could fit your bathroom tiling job into his schedule after next week. Give him a call and set it up. I'll finish installing the new subflooring next Saturday."

She lifted the card. "Thank you. You're making my job here so much easier, Trigg."

"Happy to help."

"What is it that makes you and Brayden such good Rook partners?"

"We think alike. If we sat at two separate tables, playing the same hands against the same people, we'd make identical decisions."

They talked Rook strategies while they ate.

When she couldn't take another bite, she laid her chopsticks on her plate and regarded Trigg, wondering if she should ask her burning question.

On the drive to Wytheville, she'd wanted to know what had happened to Trigg and Lauren. Who knew, maybe he courted Billie Jean in Twisty Creek and Lauren in Richmond. If she planned to ask, this would be the time. They wouldn't have a face-to-face until next week.

Her heart bounced around inside her ribcage. She hid her trembling, and now sweaty, hands under the table. Was this putting herself out there, or being blatantly nosy?

She cleared her throat. "May I ask you something sort of personal?"

He pressed his lips together and wagged his head. "I was afraid this was coming."

That was unexpected. What in the world did he think she wanted to ask him?

He leaned forward, his forearms resting against the table rim. "Would it make any difference if I told you Brayden charms women and then drops them?"

Brayden? "What are you talking about?"

"Your question wasn't about what kind of guy Brayden is?"

She jerked her chin to her chest. "No."

"Oh. Then I lied. He's the best guy I know."

This was not going well.

His arms still resting against the table, he spread his hands. "So what's your question?" His dark blue eyes met her gaze.

"I wanted to know what happened between you and Lauren."

He drew back against the booth, grabbed his napkin from his lap, and dropped it on the table. "I didn't see that one coming."

Oh no. What had she opened up? "You don't have to tell me. I only asked because you seemed so happy together." Should she be completely honest? "I saw you together once in a Richmond Kroger. This past spring."

He ran his fingers through his hair. Strands stayed peaked on one side. "I think I liked it better when I thought you were asking what kind of boyfriend Brayden would make."

"Like I said, you don't have to tell me." But she really wanted to know.

He shoved his plate toward the outside table edge. "After high school, I still had it bad for Lauren. She attended Tech for a couple of years while I completed my undergraduate and pharmacy degrees at the University of California. My dad paid for my education as long as I went to school there and worked for him. I didn't see much of Lauren. I was fairly sure she was dating other guys. Even if I'd wanted to date, I had zero time." He picked up his straw casing, toyed with it, then tore off the end.

"While I was in pharmacy school, Lauren broke up with me. I wasn't surprised, but that was still a painful time for me." He'd torn the straw casing into several small pieces, and now swirled the pieces around with his finger in a tight circle on the table. "California is not my kind of place, so as soon as I got my Pharm. D. I came back and accepted a job in Richmond. A few months later, Lauren moved to Richmond to work as a receptionist in a beauty salon. We started dating again. I was happy." He swept his straw confetti off the table into his hand and deposited the pieces on his plate. "That's probably when you saw us."

She gave a slight nod.

"After six months, I got down on one knee and asked her to marry me. She said yes. I was euphoric. Then two months later, she broke it off and kept the diamond ring. So there you have it. That happened about two months ago."

"I'm sorry, Trigg." The words barely squeaked past the lump in her throat.

"I'm doing better than I expected. I think God alerted me to Gram's problems to get my mind off my own." Their server brought the check and left it on the table. "Truth is, I've enjoyed hanging out with you this week. Last night, I was worried my buddy Brayden had swept you off your feet, and I'd have no one here to do things with on the weekends." He drained his soda and placed the glass on the table next to his plate. "So, has he?"

"Uh— Um … Brayden's a really nice guy—"

"Oooh." Trigg made a face.

"What?"

"Come on, Marge. 'A really nice guy' is the last phrase any guy wants to hear."

"What's wrong with telling the truth? You're a nice guy—"

"Aaah!" He raised his arms to ward off imaginary darts.

"I didn't know you cowboys were so touchy."

"Only when it comes to the nice-guy phrase." He rested his hands on the table. "Let's forget about how you feel about Brayden—and me. I'll take it you're available to do things with me on the weekends. Is that true?"

Even if Brayden hadn't given her a time, she'd indicated she'd be available for a date. "Brayden and I may be going out to dinner Saturday night."

He raked his fingers off the table. "The sly fox."

Goose bumps rose on her arms.

Whoa. He hung out with Billie Jean on the weekends. What did he need her for?

He edged his cell up from his pocket, then pushed it back. "It's getting late. I better go. I like to drive as much as I can in daylight, especially since more snow may fall."

Wait a minute. What about Billie Jean? The question stormed her clamped lips.

"I pay at the counter." He scooped up the check. "I need to make a pit stop at the men's room. So I'll meet you up front." Trigg made his way through the occupied tables to the restrooms.

Nooo. She couldn't wait a whole week. What was the truth about his relationship with Billie Jean!

9

CANDACE SIPPED HER MORNING COFFEE as she alternated her attention between the red curtain panels draped over the rocker and Grammy's frilly white curtains hanging on ugly white rods. Why hadn't she thought to buy fancy rods while she was in Wytheville? Because she'd been wrapped up in Trigg's desire to hang out with her on weekends and why he wouldn't be doing that with Billie Jean.

Making a Lowe's trip today would take a chunk out of her workday. Now that her vacation week was over, she needed to work on Dan Bailey's project.

Had the snowplows uncovered the roads to Galax yet? She wandered to the side window for a look at the snow depth. Whoa! Miss M was halfway to Candace's house. The elderly woman moved like a sloth as she carried a foil-covered dish and raised and lowered her rubber boots into five inches of snow.

Candace ran to the back mudroom, kicked off her moccasins, and tugged on her snow boots. No time to grab a coat. What if Miss M lost her balance and fell? The snow wasn't deep enough to fully cushion a fall. Candace clomped through the house and out the front door.

On the porch, she squelched her urgency and casually descended the stairs. "What are you bringing over, Miss Mildred?" She spoke loudly in case Miss M wasn't wearing her hearing aids.

"A cinnamon coffee cake hot out of the oven." She wore oven mitts and carried a glass baking dish with both hands.

Candace plowed through snow to Miss M. "How about you give me the coffee cake and hold on to my arm."

"Dish is too hot."

That was a problem. She couldn't grasp the rectangular dish with her bare hands. Miss M couldn't set it across her arms. Candace's long-sleeved T-shirt wouldn't protect her arms from burning. Why hadn't she grabbed her coat?

"Okay. You carry the coffee cake and I'll steady you." Candace snaked her bare hand between Miss M's upper arm and bodice and hugged the woman to her side. They planted one step after another until they reached the porch steps. "Will you promise me you'll stand right here until I get my oven mitts?"

Miss M nodded, straining to catch her breath.

"I'll be back in a jiff." Candace climbed the steps and entered the house in double time. She grabbed her mitts from a kitchen drawer and was back at Miss M's side in less than two minutes. "Okay," she said as she donned her mitts. "Hand that yummy-smelling hot baby to me."

Miss M transferred the dish. Candace set it on the porch Adirondack chair, then helped Miss M up the stairs, into the house, and onto Grammy's rocker.

For a woman who'd refused to go outside her house, Miss M had picked the worst day to show she didn't suffer from the fear-of-leaving-the-house phobia. So, this kind of risky behavior was why Trigg was concerned.

While Miss M rested, Candace took the coffee cake into the kitchen and placed two generous servings on Grammy's dessert plates. She placed steaming mugs of coffee beside the plates and escorted Miss M to the kitchen.

Candace held Miss M's hands and thanked the Lord for the cake and Miss M's safety.

Miss M sipped her coffee. "I know you think I'm a crazy old woman, but the house seemed awful quiet this morning without Trigg. I needed some company, and now that you're so close, I thought you'd like some breakfast." She set her coffee mug on the table. "I guess I'd forgotten how far apart we lived, and the snow was deeper than I thought. I turned to go back but realized I was closer to your house."

"Well, you're safe now." Candace reached across the table and patted Miss M's hand, then took a bite of cake. "I'm happy for your company, and this coffee cake is scrumptious."

Miss M nodded toward the doorway to the rest of the house. "While I was sitting in your living room, I noticed how much you've done to the room."

"I fear Grammy is tsk-tsking up in heaven."

"Oh, honey, Thelma would love it. You've got her floors gleaming. She'd been meaning to have someone redo them. Looks like a fresh coat of paint on the trim in here. It all looks real good."

"You're kind, Miss Mildred."

"Maybe you'll get the house to the way you like it and decide to stay." Miss M's eyes rounded behind her glasses.

"I don't know about that. My job is in Richmond."

"I thought you were working from here."

"Well, yes. But I can't do that full time." Well, she probably could, but …

Miss M nodded. "I wished I'd seen more of Trigg on his week off."

Candace's heart sank. "I'm so sorry I let him come over and help me."

"No, I'm not talking about you." A coy smile tipped up Miss M's lips. "I wouldn't mind if he spent a lot more time with you. I daydream about you two hitting it off."

Warmth oozed over Candace's shoulders like honey. "You do?"

"I sure do."

"I'm still sorry about Trigg being with me so much."

Miss M waved the thought away. "I'm talking about Billie Jean. He's too tenderhearted. Billie Jean and her no-good boyfriend broke up, and it was not a pretty picture."

Candace's jaw slacked and her eyes widened.

Miss M lifted her coffee mug. "Billie Jean was scared Everett would beat her up, so Trigg stayed with her while Everett moved out. Then the two of them packed her things. She couldn't afford the apartment by herself, so he helped her move back home."

"I have to be truthful, Miss Mildred. I thought Billie Jean and Trigg were dating."

"Pffft. Billie Jean's been after Trigg ever since Lauren left. He sees her as immature and puts up with the girl."

Whoa. Trigg tolerated Billie Jean, and Lauren had left him for good. Trigg was free. And Miss M dreamed she and Trigg would become an item. Which made perfect sense. They both lived in Richmond.

Miss M pressed crumbs together on her plate with her fork. "I wish with all my heart that Trigg would take a pharmacist position in Galax, Wytheville, Sparta, or one of them other towns near here." She looked at Candace. "Sometimes I see openings advertised in the newspapers for pharmacists in nearby cities. Every time, I yearn for Trigg to apply. But he doesn't. No positions have come up since Lauren called off their engagement, but I keep checking the papers all the same, hoping a pharmacist position opens." She set the fork down. "Nothing's holding him in the city now."

Except maybe, possibly, hopefully Candace Parks.

***

Minutes before midnight, Candace sat on her bed and, for the sixth time, reworded her email to Trigg. Boy, a narrow line existed between spying on Miss M and keeping Trigg informed about his grandmother. She'd done the right thing, though. She'd kept in confidence that Miss M felt lonely without Trigg. Miss M would tell him herself if she wanted him to know.

Candace hovered the cursor over Send. She'd reread it one more time.

Hey Trigg,

I hope you had an uneventful trip home yesterday. Thanks again for lunch.

Here's my Miss Mildred report:

1. This morning about eight-thirty she walked over to my house through five inches of snow, carrying a hot coffee cake. I didn't see her until she'd made it more than half way to my house. I helped her the rest of the way. Although walking to my house was dangerous, the good news is she's finally left her house.

2. Before you get riled up, in her defense, part way over, she said she realized what she'd done was foolish. But she was wise to continue on to my house when she realized it was closer. We sat, ate coffee cake, and talked about an hour. I asked her why she didn't call me before walking over. She said the paper you put on the refrigerator with my number was no longer there. She didn't want to waste the coffee cake while it was hot, so she

decided to bring it to me.

3. The missing note worried me a bit. I took her home in my car, and I went inside on the pretense of getting your telephone number. No paper with my number clung to the refrigerator. I wondered if she'd taken it off and forgotten where she put it. Then I looked under the refrigerator. I saw a paper, which I drew out with a ruler. The magnet was under the table. Trigg, that was a big piece of paper for such a wimpy magnet. She probably walked by and the magnet flew off. So I'm more worried about your mind than hers. :0)

4. She made a comment she said she'll tell you, so I think it's okay to share it. I quote, "If Trigg hadn't sold my car, I'd have driven the coffee cake to your house. Maybe he could get me one of them little ATV trucks so I can drive to your house."

5. She invited me to have breakfast with her every weekday morning. I feel like a moocher, but she was so thrilled when I said yes, I can graciously be a parasite until mid-February. I'll take work breaks and check in with her in the afternoons and early evenings as I did today. She's such a sweetheart. She keeps the later visits short, because, and I quote: "I know you're working on your computer for your company."

End of Miss Mildred report.

I need to go to Lowe's to get some good-looking curtain rods. I wish Felix were here to help me choose the best ones.

Until tomorrow's report, goodnight.

Candace, aka Marge.

Maybe she should delete the part about Felix.

Maybe that put her too far out there. She rubbed her finger across her lips and reread that last part. Cousin Addison sat on her shoulder saying, "Push Send." She did.

Her bed was covered with papers, her work laptop, and her personal one. She put her work laptop on the bedside table and stacked the papers on top. As she reached to close her personal laptop, a notification blipped. Trigg.

Her heart bounced off her stomach.

Hi Marge,

Thanks for all you did for Gram today. I'm hopeful about her getting out, but what she did was downright scary. I take full responsibility for the wimpy magnet. I'm squashing the ATV idea. And I miss you too, Marge. Felix

**

Candace called Addison.

Addison answered on the first ring. "Finally."

"And how are you?"

"I promised myself I wouldn't call you while you're on your retreat, but I thought you'd call me."

"Here I am."

"Tell me everything."

Candace rolled her eyes. "Like what?"

Addison huffed. She was silent for a moment. "Tell me five significant things that have happened since you arrived in Twisty Creek."

"I've made big progress in fixing up Grammy's

house."

"Hurray! Okay, number two."

"I'm enjoying my friendship with Miss Mildred next door."

"Aww. Do you remember when I was six and you were five she babysat us at Grammy's house and showed us how to make jigsaw puzzles out of our drawings?"

"We pasted our pictures on the back of cardboard first."

"Yeah. Number three."

Candace pictured Addison's hand with three fingers raised.

"Miss Mildred's grandson, Trigg, and his best friend, Brayden, have been helping me with Grammy's house."

"Ooh. Sounds promising for one of your passion goals. Am I right?"

Yes. Trigg was free and he missed her. "I hang out with them some."

"Love it. And four?"

"I gave you four. Spending time with the guys."

Addison let out a sigh. "I'll accept that as four, but five better be something significant."

"I still can't go into Grammy's bedroom."

***

Candace traversed the melting snow to her house from Miss M's, her stomach bulging with egg, cheese, and bacon casserole. She might finally gain hips at the rate Miss M shelled out the calories. Tuesday, it'd been blueberry waffles. Yesterday's cherry crepes were her favorite.

She let herself inside her house. If she hadn't fallen for Miss M before she left Twisty Creek five years ago, she had now. Her surrogate grandmother was as kind and entertaining as Grammy.

As sweet as Miss M was, she was not happy about Trigg selling her car. But that didn't give Candace the right to include Miss M's frequent comments about her lack of transportation in the daily reports to Trigg. The two Aldermans would have to work that problem out on their own. Her job was to provide Miss M a listening ear.

And her listening ear seemed to be working wonders. Miss M decided to teach her favorite dessert recipes to Candace before she returned to Richmond. The lessons had started yesterday. She now excelled at rolling out dough for an apple pie crust.

No way would she return to Richmond and fall out of touch with Miss M this time. And she'd make the four-hour trip occasionally to visit her on weekends— perhaps with Trigg.

Ah, Trigg. She climbed the stairs and sat at the desk in her bedroom. As she opened her work laptop, her gaze drifted to the printed copy of his email response to her Monday report. She'd circled, "I miss you too, Marge" in red ink and taped the paper to a framed photo on the desk. A smile tugged her lips. His words did more for her spirits than the photo underneath, which showed her at age ten sitting beside her prize-winning pumpkin.

He'd be back late tonight. Tomorrow, three would sit at Miss M's breakfast table. An hour later, as she and Miss M had agreed, to give Trigg a chance for a good night's sleep.

Mirroring her workdays to Trigg's functioned well. Mainly because she didn't need to work ten-hour days and had time to work on the house and visit Miss M. As her boss said, she was a natural programmer. She could see trails of code in her mind like a chess player could foresee several moves and possible scenarios. Working from home also cut down on the interruptions. She could get used to working at home all year-round.

Trigg kept pushing for a scheduled nightly phone call, but then she wouldn't be able hit the delete button on the words she'd rather not say. Nothing new about that. She'd always had a hard time weeding through her thoughts to find something worthwhile to say. It was easier to stay mum or write a text or email.

She looked at the circled words on Trigg's email. He seemed to understand her. Before she'd realized the truth, he knew she'd meant she missed him when she'd written about needing help choosing curtain rods. He may not rank as Miss M's hero right now, but he sure could push Candace's talk button. Maybe passion was less about particular feelings and more about the satisfaction of being the person God called you to be.

10

CANDACE PASSED TRIGG THE PLATTER of bacon and sausage links.

Miss Mildred set a plate stacked with pecan pancakes on a hot pad and sat at the table. "There's more batter, so eat as many pancakes as you want."

Trigg had already dressed in his work attire, open flannel shirt over T-shirt, jeans, and work boots. His hair stuck up in places, and whiskers shadowed his jaw. He slapped butter on a column of five pancakes. "I'm going to get the bathroom subfloor replaced today. What do you plan to tackle, Candace?"

"I bought handsome bronze rods for the new curtain panels and plan to hang curtains in the rooms where I've finished painting the wood trim."

Miss M drizzled maple syrup over her pancakes. "What're you going to hang today, honey? I didn't catch that."

Candace spoke louder. "Curtain panels."

"Oh. How lovely."

"Are your hearing aids in, Gram?"

"They make my ear canals itch. I'll put them in later. Candace, you be sure to come for dinner tonight.

Pork chops in mushroom gravy. Did I mention that my driver's license is still good? Candace makes a flaky pie crust now."

Candace darted her gaze to Trigg. Should she stifle a chuckle at Miss M's method of expressing her gripes or fear the gray-haired lady had fired the first battle shot?

Trigg paused, his fork laden with a dripping pancake portion halfway to his mouth. "Do you have a list under the table, Gram, that suddenly needed airing?"

"*Someone* called me only once this week, and if I don't spit out what I've had to store up for the week, I forget. You know how my brain gets addled."

He laughed. "Nothing's wrong with your brain, Gram." He downed the bite and speared another. "We'd better get busy on your house, Candace."

"I wish I could drive over to see your progress." Miss M sipped her coffee. "But I guess I'll have to wait until Candace can carry me over next week."

He stood. "I'll drive you over later today." He tugged on the ball cap he'd hung on his chair post and took his plate and coffee mug to the sink.

Miss M waved him off. "Leave the dishes to me."

He bent over and kissed her cheek. "We'll be back for lunch. We can all go to the diner."

"No. Candace brought me salad fixin's from Food City, and I'm making a Cobb salad from leftovers. No need to eat out."

***

Candace drilled the last screw into the rod holder and hung the last curtain panel in the living room. She descended the ladder, stood in the doorway to the dining room, and admired her work. The accent wall on either side of the fireplace finished in laminate flooring, the light taupe paint, white trim, and red curtain panels took years off the room. The furniture would arrive next week.

She poured two glasses of sweet tea and climbed the stairs to the bathroom. Trigg had made a lot of noise this morning. Her ears still rang from his hammering and drilling.

Tea glasses in hand, she stood in the bathroom doorway. "How about a short break?"

He looked up from where he knelt on new subflooring. "Sounds good."

They sat on the hardwood floor in the hallway side by side, leaning against the wall. He downed half his tea in one long draw.

"Trigg, couldn't Miss Mildred have a small car that's easy to get into and out of and to park? Maybe she'd promise to wear her hearing aids and drive no farther than the minimart, diner, church, and friends' homes. Maybe she could even go as far as Food City in Independence. That's an easy drive."

His arms anchored on his tented knees and the glass suspended from his fingertips, he regarded her face. Wheels turned behind his gorgeous blue eyes.

He rested his head back against the wall and swirled his tea. "She doesn't go to church. She has friends willing to take her wherever she wants to go."

Candace turned and rested a shoulder to the wall to face him. "I know you worry about her, Trigg. But she gets around well, is of sound mind, spots a fly on the wall, and is only eighty. She has friends much older than she is who drive."

He rotated his head toward her. "But she doesn't need to drive. She signed the papers when I sold her car." He started to rise.

Candace grabbed his arm. "Look at me." He sat and gave her his attention. "I'm no psychologist, but I think Miss Mildred refuses to go to church because she's angry at you for taking away her freedom to go places. She doesn't leave her house because she's protesting your decision. It's like she's saying, 'If you want me to be a shut-in, I'll be a shut-in.' If she didn't need to eat or bake for her own enjoyment, she probably wouldn't allow anyone to buy her groceries."

He stared at her. For a long time. Was he calculating what tone to use to tell her to butt out of his business?

His lips crept into a smile. "You should be a psychologist, Marge. I'd never have figured that out myself. But I think you're right. Gram's at war." He grasped a strand of her hair that had escaped her ponytail and placed it behind her ear. "Let me think on it."

He finished off his tea and set the glass on the floor. "Here's another problem for you, Miss Psychologist. Gram only goes down and up the stairs once a day. It's a painful trip. She takes her afternoon nap on the living room couch. I could convert the dining room into a bedroom and move her downstairs, but there's only a half bath on the first floor. I've found a couple that takes in one or two people into their ranch home and assists them as needed. Gram would have company and no more stairs."

Blood drained from Candace's face. He might as well slit Miss M's throat. How could Trigg switch from considering a car for his grandmother to writing her death sentence? Stay in reasoning mode. Don't scream at him. Think.

He gave her a one-sided grin. "This one's not so easy, huh."

It was as easy as Miss M's apple pie. An idea hit her. She rose to her knees and sat back on her heels, her heart pounding hallelujahs at her solution. "How about you sell Miss Mildred's house and lease mine? I have the downstairs bedroom and full bath Grammy and Grandpa added after his arthritis got bad. My kitchen is just as good as hers, maybe better. I'm having a new refrigerator delivered and installed next week. She'll have more room to store her cold baking ingredients. My house is in the same neighborhood, and she's familiar with its floor plan." She poked his arm. "And I'll lease it to you for a dollar a year."

His stare morphed into a glare. "That's your solution?"

"It might take Miss Mildred some time to get used to Grammy's house, but I think it would work. You could stay in one of the upstairs rooms when you visit."

"You're serious."

"Dead serious."

"You're ready to rent it to her for a dollar a year?"

"Yes. Then you could use the money from her house to take care of her in her actual old age."

"You can't lease your house for a dollar."

"Oh yes I can. I've let the house sit for five years without a penny's rent from the resident mice. Plus, I know I don't look it, but I'm rich." If only she could take a picture of his blank expression. "Now don't start getting all sweet on me for my money."

"You're rich." A deadpan statement.

"Yes. When my parents and sister, Jules, died in the car accident when I was ten, my parents were heavily insured and had accidental death riders. I received over a million dollars that was put in a trust fund. Grandpa had a booming construction business here in Twisty Creek because people wanted him to build them houses with drywall. And Grammy had hundreds of acres of land. My cousin, Addison, and I inherited land and a good chunk of money after Grammy's death. I've had help investing my money wisely." She raised her forefinger. "Plus, I sock away my annual bonuses for holding my company's number-one, hotshot programmer position. I live in an average cost apartment and haven't desired to spend my money until fixing up this house. I've loved doing that." She emphasized her last words with raised open hands.

Trigg gaped, but she wasn't finished.

"I've planned to marry and use my savings for a modest house for six. I've earmarked part of my savings for college funds for my four children, family educational trips, and generous giving. I hope to quit my job and be a stay-at-home mom. We'll see how that plays out. So I don't need the money from Grammy's house." She snapped her fingers. "And one more benefit if Miss Mildred rented my house. My cousin would be off my back. She'd be relieved that someone is living in Grammy's house treating it with loving care." She chuckled. "You might want to shut your gaping mouth. A few flies zipped inside the house when I brought in supplies."

He closed his mouth, then wagged his head, grinning. "That's the most fantastic story I've ever heard. I'll have to think a long, long time on your proposal."

Because it would hurt his guy ego to have the help?

"And don't go thinking I'm too proud to accept a rich woman's charity." He touched her nose. "I'd accept anything to make Gram's life better."

He'd read her mind? Wasn't that proof they belonged together? In Richmond?

He climbed to his feet and extended his hand. She placed hers in his, and he pulled her up.

He didn't let go. "You are one amazing woman, Candace Parks."

There. Just then. He'd glanced at her lips. Was he going to kiss her? She'd reduce the house rent to fifty cents if he'd grant her one dreamy kiss.

He raised her hand and twirled her to face the stairs. "Get back to work, Marge, or this place won't be worth a nickel."

***

Candace dried the frying pan and handed it to Trigg to put away. Miss M let the water out of the sink. If Miss M lived in Grammy's house, she'd have a dishwasher. Grandpa insisted Grammy have one installed not long before he died. The machine was still in great shape, probably because Grammy only used it once a week.

Miss M hung the dishcloth over the faucet. "It's been a good but long day. I think I'll turn in. You kids watch TV, play a game, or talk." Her gaze swung from Candace to Trigg. "Enjoy each other."

Trigg placed his hands on Miss M's shoulders and looked into her eyes. "Gram, I know you're unhappy that I sold your car. I'm thinking about a solution. Okay?"

She grasped his chin and gave it a shake. "Don't over think it, dear. The solution is simple." She left the kitchen. Groans and squeaks came from the stairs with several seconds between each step's protest.

"So, what would you like to do?" Trigg gestured toward the living room. "The TV is in here."

She wandered in and stood before the painting on the wall next to the TV. The artist's pastoral scene could've been the view behind Miss M's house. Candace studied the pasture, cows, and mountains. Her heart rate seemed to slow and she couldn't help smiling. The painting would be ideal in her apartment, to remind her of the gorgeous southwest Virginia scenery and to brighten her bare walls. Now that she was Miss Interior Decorator, maybe she'd give her apartment some TLC.

She rotated on the balls of her feet, smiled at Trigg, and looked around the room. A similar painting graced the opposite wall.

Trigg slid his hands into his pants pockets. "Do you like the mountain paintings?"

"Very much."

"Granddaddy took up painting after he retired. Those two are his. I have one at my place in Richmond, and several more are stored in the basement. Would you like one?"

"You're kidding."

He shook his head.

"I'd love one. To remember Twisty Creek."

"I'll check with Gram, but I'm ninety-nine percent positive she'll want you to have one."

"I'd pay for one."

He frowned. "You've gotten too citified, Marge."

"Then I humbly would accept one. If Miss Mildred would like me to own one." Should she sit on the sofa?

"Sit on the sofa." Trigg aimed the remote at the TV. "It's hard to see the TV from the armchairs."

Like her, he'd showered and dressed up a bit. The crisp, blue-checkered shirt tucked into his jeans sat well on his broad shoulders.

She maneuvered between the coffee table and the sofa, kicked off her black ballet flats, and sat, tucking one leg beneath her.

An HGTV show popped onto the screen. Trigg chuckled. "Looks like Gram has been watching fixer-upper shows."

"Don't change the channel. I like this show. A couple travels to some foreign land to buy a house. The realtor shows them three, then they have to choose one. It's fun to decide the place that's best for them and see if they pick that house."

He sidled between the table and the sofa, turning down the TV volume from where Miss Mildred had it set, and sat next to her. He pulled off his boots and set them on the rug at his side of the sofa.

The narrator informed viewers the couple had given up their jobs in Des Moines, Iowa, to purchase a house in Costa Rica. The redheaded mother of two wanted an open floor plan, a modern kitchen, and a place near the beach. The tall, mild-mannered husband wanted a house with tropical flair, close to restaurants and shops, minutes from his new bank job, and under their budget.

Trigg pushed the coffee table farther from the couch and set his stocking feet on its surface. "You know who's going to get her way, don't you?"

"Yeah, probably, but you never know. Some people surprise you."

"Don't I know it." He tugged her hair.

She rolled her eyes.

The realtor showed the couple House One, attempting to please the woman.

"With that ocean view, they'd be crazy not to choose that place." Candace accepted a stick of gum Trigg offered.

"Yeah, but did you see how his face caved when the realtor said the price was five thousand over budget. And it's forty minutes from his job."

Candace crushed the gum between her teeth and was surprised the mint flavor she expected tasted like … "Watermelon?"

He arched an eyebrow at her. "Marge, if you don't like watermelon gum, we're over."

She could learn to like watermelon-flavored gum. "It's okay, but I draw the line at avocado."

On the TV, the woman gushed over the modern house. The husband didn't say much.

House Two ticked all the husband's boxes. With a brightened countenance, he walked through the house nodding.

The show went to a commercial.

"Man. How can you watch a show where the poor guy isn't going to get his way?" He directed a hand toward the TV. "He really likes House Two. It's on budget and close to work."

"Would you give up the first house's ocean view and a three-minute walk to the beach? Why bother moving to Costa Rica?"

He cocked his head and pursed his lips. "You're right. Why move to a tropical island and buy a house that's just like one you could buy in Richmond?"

"Remember, she has to live in that house all day with two young children. It'd be better if she could walk them to the beach."

The show came on. House Three sat atop a hill, had a ten minute-drive to the beach, sported tropical colors, wood floors and trim, offered a limited view of the ocean from the deck, and was two thousand under budget. The woman thought the kitchen was too small. The husband's drive to work was only ten minutes, but he wished the house were closer to the town's center.

When the show went to a commercial, Trigg muted the sound. "I think House Three is a good compromise. They want to stick with one car. He'll have to get a bicycle or motorbike, but that wouldn't be bad."

"I'm not so sure." Candace drew up both legs under her and faced him. "She's going to have to pack the kids up and drive to the beach. I think they'll go with

House One. After all, she gave up nearness to her family to follow him to Costa Rica."

"Oh, come on. He's offering her a once-in-a-life-time adventure."

She crossed her arms over her ribcage. "Yeah, big adventure with two small children to deal with all day."

"Okay, let's make a wager. Whoever votes for the house the couple selects can choose what we do next."

"I hope you're as good at gin rummy as you are at Rook."

"I hope you're as good at …" He chuckled. "You'll have to wait to find out what you'll be doing next. I say they'll choose House Three."

"House One."

The show was back. Trigg unmuted the TV.

The couple sat at a picnic table next to the beach, sipping tropical concoctions.

They aired their reasons for their personal choices, she for House One and he for House Two. The husband said he could compromise and go with House Three.

"As much as I love the first house and the beach," the woman said, "I'd rather you didn't spend forty minutes commuting each way so you can spend more time with us."

The husband's eyes lit up. "Then House Three?"

She nodded, and they kissed.

"Yes!" Trigg pumped a fist. "I win." He directed

the remote at the TV, and the screen went black. He grinned at her, then raised and lowered his eyebrows.

If the guy who created games in Lowe's came up with an embarrassing game, she'd slip into her ballet flats and go home.

She scrunched her face. "What do I have to do?"

"Now, don't be a sore loser." He touched her knee with a forefinger. "It's what are *we* going to do?"

"Just so you know. I have my limits."

"You'd renege on a bet? Fair is fair. I'd have graciously beat you in gin rummy."

"Ha, ha."

He stood, crossed to the TV console, and opened the cabinet. His long legs folded into a squat, and he hunted inside.

What in the world was he going to make her do? He'd better not pull out the old game in which you had to twist around each other to touch the right colored spot on a mat.

Trigg stood and lifted a CD. "Gram loves the Bee Gees."

"Really?" She laughed. "Good for her."

He inserted the disc into the CD player next to the TV.

If his idea was for her to lip-sync a Bee Gee song, she was out of here. She slipped her toe into a ballet flat.

As "Too Much Heaven" played, he turned and extended his hand toward her. "May I have this dance?"

Oh my. Her legs felt wobbly, and she hadn't even stood yet.

"Come on, Marge, pay up."

She removed her toe from her shoe, stood, and placed her hand in his warm fingers. Once she cleared the coffee table, he pulled her toward him in one smooth movement. She placed her hand on his shoulder, and he curled her other hand to his chest. The top of her head fit below his chin.

Oh my, oh my. How could he not feel her heart pummeling his chest?

He danced her around the rug. When they moved too close to the coffee table, he shoved the table to the couch with his foot. Then he spun her out and reeled her back.

Her heart was no longer under her control. Oh, don't let the tune stop too soon.

He slid his hand up her back and tugged a handful of her hair until she looked up at him. Was this the moment? Was she going to taste his lips for more than a second?

He grinned. "You make a good dance partner." He looked at her lips, then spun her out.

The song stopped. As another song began, he gently pulled her back to him and stood still.

His head tilted down toward hers. Oh my. Her toes curled into the rug.

The loud ring of Miss Mildred's landline blared,

surely at the top volume setting.

Trigg lunged for the handset on an end table. "Hello." He cupped his forehead with his free hand. "There was a reason for that, Cindy." His voice was flat. He listened for a moment. "Hold on." He put his hand over the receiver. "It's the pharmacy. Since my cell service doesn't work here, I had to give this as my alternate number." He nodded to the handset. "She's the new pharmacist technician on the night shift." His eyebrows moved together in a painful look. "This is going to take awhile."

Candace reached for her shoes under the coffee table. "That's okay. I'd better head home."

The painful look deepened. "Don't go."

If he only knew how bad she wanted to stay. But a strong pressure was telling her to go. "I've enjoyed myself." She dropped her flats to the rug and wriggled her feet into her shoes. "I'll see you tomorrow. Miss Mildred is teaching me how to make fudge."

She lifted her hand and left him standing with his hand over the receiver and those kissable lips set in a pout.

11

CANDACE TOWELED HER FACE IN the downstairs bathroom. If the tiling job went well, the upstairs bath would be done by the end of next week. Boy, did her face look rosy. Because she'd rubbed the towel too roughly against her skin, or was it the bloom of L-O-V-E—love?

She flipped the light switch and left the bathroom. At the staircase, she placed her foot on the first step. "He loves me." She climbed to the next step. "He loves me not." She continued up the stairs, alternating the ditties. Just before the landing, she stopped. If she ascended the next step, she'd end on *He loves me not.* Was the upstairs floor an actual step? Wasn't the stair she stood on the last one, and he loved her?

She rolled her eyes. What was she, a lovesick teenager? Maybe not, but how could she sleep if she kept replaying tonight's dance with Trigg?

As she crawled into bed, something niggled her. Oh yes. Why had she felt the pressure to go home tonight instead of staying until Trigg finished his call? She wouldn't have let anything happen beyond kisses. She'd made promises to God. Affection progressed beyond kisses after marriage.

She sat cross-legged with a pillow in her lap.

Or was the jab to her conscience because of her date with Brayden tomorrow night? How could she be ready to sign on as Trigg's forever woman, then go out with another guy? Not fair to either cowboy.

Great. Forget drifting off to sleep recalling her heart beating against Trigg's as they danced. No. She'd have a sleepless night, churning over how she could last through a date with Brayden, knowing she was wasting his time and money. She had to do the right thing. But what was that?

***

Candace admired the plate of fudge cubes gracing Miss M's kitchen counter. "I feel guilty that Trigg's worked on my bathroom all afternoon while we giggled, laughed, and made fudge."

Miss M waved her away. "Just think how pleased he'll be to enjoy the fudge when he gets home."

"I guess. The house is almost ready to put on the market."

Except Grammy's room. Entering her haven and freshening up paint had to be done next week, or Candace wouldn't be able to put the house on the market her last week in Twisty Creek.

She looked up from wrapping the plate of fudge in cellophane. Miss M's lips drooped.

Why had she said that? She knew Miss M didn't want her to sell the house and go home to Richmond.

But maybe it was better to prepare her friend for reality. Candace circumvented the table cluttered with fudge-making pans, bowls, and wooden spoons and hugged her friend. "I'll come back to visit, Miss Mildred. I promise."

"I know you will, honey. But it's not the same as having you here so I can visit with you for a few minutes every day—like I visited your grandmother."

The front door opened and shut. Trigg was here.

He entered the kitchen. "All done. Your bathroom floor is ready to tile."

Miss M gestured toward the plate of fudge. "And here's your reward."

"Let me wash up, and then I'll see if your fudge lives up to a half day of hard labor." He strode out of the kitchen.

Miss M ran hot water into one of the double sinks. "You're learning so many luscious recipes, Candace, a man would be thrilled to have you as his wife." She nodded toward the doorway through which Trigg had left.

Candace gave Miss M a shy smile.

"You two could get married, leave those jobs in Richmond, move back here, and live in that fixer-upper next door."

"I don't—"

Trigg clomped into the kitchen. "Let me at the fudge."

Candace looked at the kitchen wall clock sporting a

picture of a different bird at each number. "Oh my, I need to leave."

Miss M raised her eyebrows in alarm. "Why?"

Trigg licked fudge from his thumb, then crossed his arms over his chest and leveled a gaze on Candace. "Because she's got a hot date with Brayden."

Talk about hot. Candace's face flamed.

Miss M stopped drying a bowl. "Our Brayden?"

"Yep."

Miss M turned a confused face to Candace.

Did Benedict Arnold ever feel this guilty? "We made the date a week ago."

"Oh." Miss M pressed her lips together as if she were imprisoning a comment she knew better not to spring.

***

Candace stood at the window fingering aside a red panel. She wouldn't allow Brayden to come to the door. She glanced over at Miss M's house. Were she and Trigg standing in the living room peering out the window? Maybe being invisible had its advantages. The past two weeks she'd done a bang-up job of putting herself out there and garnering dates. But she'd also distressed Miss M and disgruntled Trigg.

She bit her lip to stop a smile from creeping onto her lips. Perhaps a little jealousy was good for the guy who'd always had women fainting at his feet.

Except Lauren.

Ugh. So, now she was going to pile the guilt for enjoying jilted Trigg's jealousy on top of the guilt she already suffered for letting Brayden take her on a date? Seemed unfair.

Car lights appeared over the rise in the road, illuminated her driveway, then swept onto its gravel. She grabbed her handbag and hurried outside.

Unfortunately, date-like, Brayden stood at her door and held it open. She glanced at Miss M's living room windows. No cracks between the curtains. Should she feel slighted?

"Hi." Brayden nodded toward her. "You look pretty."

"Hey." She climbed into his truck, then watched the handsome cowboy skirt the front of the truck. *Lord, give me courage.*

Brayden climbed into the truck and started the engine. "How was your Saturday?"

She'd practiced being a traitor all day. "Miss M taught me how to make fudge."

"Did you bring me some?"

"As a matter of fact, I did." She patted her handbag. "I'm taking care of dessert tonight."

He chuckled as he backed out of the driveway. "Fudge will make a good midnight snack. I'm buying the whole spread tonight." His eyes twinkled in the lights from the dash.

With the difficult task ahead, she had no appetite for anything. Not even fudge.

They approached the elementary school. "Would you turn into the parking lot there?" She pointed ahead at the school.

He sent her a worried look and slowed the truck. "I don't think the building is open."

Oh no. He thought she was up to her escaping-from-his-truck-to-find-a-bathroom routine. "I just want to talk a minute."

He parked in a space and killed the engine.

She would not say the kiss-of-death word. Not on her life, even if he was one of the nicest guys she'd ever met. "I can't let you take me to dinner."

He shifted to face her. The light from the one streetlamp nearer the building lit his wrinkled forehead. He remained quiet, waiting for her to continue.

"Since last week, I ... I ..."

"... have fallen for Trigg." His voice came soft with a hint of either understanding or disappointment.

Actually, her falling had happened in high school. But Brayden didn't need to know details. "The dumb thing is, I don't even know if he returns my feelings." Trigg's jealous announcement at Miss M's hadn't necessarily meant Trigg was falling in love. His resentment could've been because he'd thought he'd lost a contest to his best friend.

So now she was guilty of breaking up best friends?

Brayden ran his hand down his face. "Trigg and I've been friends since kindergarten. Best friends since middle school."

And now she'd wedged their friendship apart.

"I know him well." He tapped the steering wheel. "I'm going to tell you the truth about Trigg."

No. Don't do it. Don't be one of those guys who betrays his best friend and brandishes all his faults. Stay the nice guy.

"You won't find a nicer guy."

She curbed a burst of laughter. She'd have a talk with Trigg about the nice-guy terminology, because Brayden had just branded Trigg with the nice-guy curse. Or did Brayden mean what he said?

"Could you expand on that?"

"He's a man of integrity. His yes is yes and his no is no. Oh, he likes to have fun with people." Brayden scratched his head. "He's got the knack for kidding that I'll never have, but he's a loyal friend. I've always counted on him and he's never failed me. That's what I'm getting at."

"So are you saying I should fall for him?"

"I'm saying if he's given you signs that he likes you, then he truly likes you. And he's been through a silo full of hurt lately. So if you aren't sure how you feel about him, don't get his hopes up."

Wham! Just because putting herself out there had gained interest from a couple of guys, everything was not about the poor, invisible girl. Thank heavens, Brayden couldn't see her red face.

Brayden and Trigg were the definition of best

friends. She gulped down her embarrassment. "Even if nothing comes of a romantic relationship between Trigg and me, I hope I can be as good a friend to him as you are to each other." She touched his arm. Dare she use the forbidden word, even if she meant it? Sure. "You're a nice guy too."

Brayden nodded and started the engine. "Will you at least allow me to buy you a burger and fries? My belly's running on empty."

"Sure. I'm hungry for a juicy hamburger and ketchup-covered fries." And she was.

***

"Thank you for a delicious dinner, Brayden."

Brayden turned the truck out of the fast-food lot. "Are you serving your gourmet dessert?"

"*Certainement.*" She opened her handbag, dug out a freezer bag containing two large cubes of fudge, and handed him the bigger one. "*Bon appeitit.*"

He bit into the fudge. "Ah, *magnifique.*" He looked at her. "Our French Three class wasn't a total waste."

He knew they'd been in her French class together. Maybe she'd been too hard on Trigg about giving his friends a script to welcome the invisible girl.

He chuckled. "I have the perfect idea for the rest of our date."

"I thought you were only taking me to dinner."

"I'd planned to take you to Lovers' Lot."

A laugh burst from her. She licked fudge from her

lips. "That would be a first for me."

"For me too." He popped the remainder of his fudge into his mouth. "But since you think I'm only a nice guy, I don't think making out among vehicles full of teens will work. I have a better idea."

"Where?"

"Not telling."

She tried playing twenty questions, but he was too tough to crack. When they pulled into Twisty Creek, all possibilities vanished from her brain. There was nothing to do in Twisty Creek, except attend functions at the firehouse, and none were scheduled this Saturday.

He turned on to Shadow Road.

"You're taking me home. Are you going to help me paint baseboards?"

"Naw."

He turned into Miss M's driveway.

"What are you doing?"

He grinned. "Let's see if Miss Mildred and someone special are up for a game of Rook."

Rook, her foot. More like opening a can of embarrassment opportunities. Was Brayden not as nice as she thought?

"Come on. It'll be fun. Trigg leaves tomorrow, and he'll be gone for a full week."

That made some sense. And Trigg had wanted to play Rook with her this weekend "to see how aggressive" she was, but ... "I'm not sure about this."

He parked behind Trigg's SUV. They left the truck and hiked to the porch.

As Brayden's fingers reached for the storm door handle, she grabbed his hand. "If we're going to drop in on them, let's do it right." She pressed the doorbell button.

After a few moments, Trigg opened the door, dressed in jeans, a long-sleeved Henley, and socks. He pushed open the storm door. "Whoa. Trick or treating passed a few months ago. But the Candace and Brayden costumes are authentic looking."

"Step aside." Brayden ushered Candace to enter. "We've come to beat you in Rook."

As she stepped inside, she looked into Trigg's eyes, which registered puzzlement. She raised her eyebrows and shoulders to say, "This was not my idea."

Miss M beamed at Brayden's proposal, shuffled her slippers from the kitchen, and returned with a deck of Rook cards. Then she filled everyone's drink orders and placed a plate stacked with fudge on the table.

Trigg and Miss M won all three games.

Brayden gathered the cards. "Sorry, Candace, they skunked us."

Candace collected glasses and took them to the sink. "It wasn't you. It was your rusty partner." Or she'd taken too many risks to prove she could be aggressive.

Miss M wrapped the leftover fudge in cellophane. "I think it was the considerable expertise of your opponents."

Trigg chuckled and put his arm around Miss M's shoulders. "I have to agree with Gram."

Candace would let that comment pass. There was always next weekend for a rematch.

"I'm beat." Brayden lifted his coat from the back of his chair. "Will you drive my date home, Trigg?"

"Sure. Let me get my boots." Trigg left the kitchen.

"I think that's a wonderful idea, Brayden." Miss M's expression brightened.

"No, no, no." Candace said, "I'll walk home. By myself."

Trigg returned. "Sorry, darlin', we can't have you attacked by a polecat."

"Or a possum." Brayden shook Candace's hand. "I enjoyed our date." A grin stretching his lips, he shrugged into his coat and headed for the front door.

Trigg sat on a kitchen chair and tugged on his boots.

The least she could do was help Miss M with the dishes. Candace grabbed a dish towel hanging over the oven handle and dried the glasses Miss M had washed and set in the drying rack. "Miss M, will you go to church with us tomorrow?" She held her breath.

"Everybody will fuss over me since I haven't been in a while."

"Let them. I want you to join me in worshiping the Lord. That's why we go to church." Candace glanced at Trigg. "Trigg and I'll be right there with you."

Miss M rinsed a glass and handed it to Candace.

"I've been wanting to go, but I was afraid people would judge me for staying home. But you're right, honey, it's not about my fears, but about worshiping God." She wrung water from the dishcloth. "I'll go."

"Good." Candace kissed Miss M's cheek and stored the dried glasses in the cupboard.

Trigg stood. "Ready?"

In Candace's drive way, they sat in Trigg's SUV, the heater humming.

She looked at the sky. Such a beautiful clear night. "You can see a million stars tonight." She sensed Trigg studying her.

"So what happened on your date with Brayden that brought you two to our house?"

"I realized I didn't want him buying me an expensive dinner when I knew I'd be going back to Richmond soon." No lie there.

"Sometimes a man just wants to enjoy a woman's company. No ulterior motives. Treating a woman to dinner doesn't mean they're signing a contract."

Was he trying to tell her something? She searched his face in the light from the porch. "Is that why you bought my lunch at the Chinese restaurant last Sunday?" She might as well face the truth before she sank too deep.

"Yes, and other reasons. And I plan to buy you lunch again tomorrow if you're willing to drive to Wytheville."

"I'm willing, if you let me buy your lunch this time.

Sometimes a girl wants to enjoy a guy's company."

"Is that why you're joining me?"

"Yes, and other reasons."

"Copycat."

She chuckled. "Any more thoughts about moving Miss Mildred into my house when I leave?"

"I'm still chawing on that one."

"I wish I could do something that would really help her."

"You have. Tonight, you gave her a great gift."

She drew back. "What gift was that?"

"You gave her a way to go back to church. I couldn't give her that gift because I violated her trust."

"She knows you have her best interests at heart."

"I know, but ever since you arrived, she's shed ten years. I could almost swear Gram's hair is less gray."

"I'm glad. She's brought a spark back in my life too."

"So, we're on for church and lunch tomorrow?" He fiddled with a strand of her hair.

"Yes. I'll drive my car, and Miss Mildred and I can leave from the church."

"I already asked. Miss Cupid said she would be too tired to go to Wytheville and would need a nap on her sofa."

"I'll still drive my car. While you take Miss Cupid home, I'll corner Randy Barnett in the church parking lot to see if my tiling job is on his schedule for next week."

"It's a plan."

She placed her hand on the door handle.

"Candace …"

She opened the door and swung her head toward him. "Yes?"

He regarded her. "Never mind."

She got out and closed the door.

He backed out of the driveway, his tires grinding gravel.

What was he about to say before "never mind"? If it was about a kiss, maybe he thought a guy didn't kiss a girl on the night of another man's date.

12

CANDACE SLIPPED INTO THE PEW beside Trigg. She leaned forward and waved at Miss M, whose eyes lit up. Trigg's Sunday-go-to-church-cologne was all male. Breathing in a scent like that, a woman might faint when she stood for the first hymn. But, of course, Trigg would hold the hymnal for Miss M. Candace would be on her own today.

The organist played two of her favorite traditional hymns, "Turn Your Eyes Upon Jesus" and "To God Be the Glory." They connected her heart to the Lord. More people populated the pews than last week, like they expected something special.

The pastor rose from his chair and moved to the lectern. "We have a special guest today to bring us the message God has laid on her heart. She's made a long trip to speak to us. Esther has been serving the Lord six years overseas. Would you please welcome Esther Little from Papua New Guinea."

Blood drained from Candace's face, and lightheadedness came over her. Her heart raced. She had to get out of the sanctuary. *Lord, please don't let Miss M be alarmed.* But if she'd didn't leave now, men would be carrying her out on a stretcher. She turned over the bulletin and grabbed a short pencil from the holder on the pew ahead of her. Her hand shook as she wrote, "Have to go. Don't follow."

Candace planted the bulletin on Trigg's knee and scurried from the church.

In her car, she drank water from the bottle she'd brought along for her trip to Wytheville. She leaned against the headrest and closed her eyes. After a moment, the lightheadedness eased. She opened her eyes. Trigg strode from the church, looking to either side. Her note had given her less of a start than she'd hoped.

She fumbled her car keys from her handbag, and as soon as the engine fired, put the car in gear, backed from the space, and left Trigg less than three strides from her side window.

On the road, she headed for the mountains. No one would be at Hale Lake this time of year. She had to be alone. A missionary from PNG speaking today was no coincidence. This was a message from God. And she had to be somewhere alone to figure out what His message meant.

She passed through Elk Creek, then turned onto the dirt road that led to the mountain lake. As her car ground gravel, images from recurring dreams invaded her mind. She was traipsing through thick PNG jungle undergrowth that reached out to trap her. She struggled to move forward, but vines wrapped around her ankles and arms.

A deer skittered across the road in front of her. She stomped on the brakes.

That did it. She jammed the gearshift into Park, dropped her hands from the steering wheel, and wailed.

After several minutes and three soggy tissues, she drove until she reached the parking area below the stones that served as stairs to the hidden lake. She turned off the engine.

Whipping another tissue from the box inside the console, she let out a groan that rumbled up from deep within her like lava from a volcano. "What does this mean, Lord?"

Until she calmed down, she wouldn't be able to think. She gripped the steering wheel with both hands and drew in deep breaths.

"Lord, the only way Ms. Little could be the guest speaker today is that you're orchestrating what I've feared all along. You're cashing in on my childhood promise. I get it. A relationship with a man and family were never Your plan. Is that why my conscience went berserk over Trigg's incoming kiss?" She ran a tissue under her runny nose. "I know in my heart You know what's best. You'll give me the passion for the work once I obey and go."

Tears flowed. "But I want a husband and family so badly, Lord. I'm so disappointed. Please help me. I can't do this without You."

She regained control, blew her nose, and got out of the car. Boy, it was cold. Her winter coat sat on the pew where she'd shrugged it off at the beginning of the service. Leaning inside the car, she extracted her keys. The blanket she'd used to cover her laptops and printer lay in the trunk. Thankfully, it had been sunny and warmer yesterday, and even in the mountains, only a few patches of snow remained. She locked the car door, and strode to the trunk, where she found the blanket and wrapped it around her shoulders. The short hike up to the lake would get her heart pumping and help keep her warm.

At the top, leafless trees and firs fringed the lake. Would it be foolish to walk the half-mile trail that encircled the manmade reservoir? Maybe she'd sit on the knoll overlooking the lake like she had years ago when she wanted to think. She tucked a corner of the blanket under her hips and sat on the hard, grassy area. While she admired the reflection of the trees and sky on the lake's glassy surface, her heart stopped racing and her breathing returned to normal.

She rocked her upper body. How did one become a missionary? She needed to research that. It probably involved applications to mission boards, training, and quitting her job. If Grammy's house didn't sell quickly, she'd have to involve Addison in that process.

She wouldn't be able to fulfill her promise to Miss M to visit her. And she'd have to dump her feelings for Trigg. The knot in her throat ached. Hopefully, God would give her peace, but handling her parents' and Jules's deaths had given her a few coping techniques of her own. Stifle passions and work so hard at school or work that she was too exhausted to grieve or care about building relationships.

***

At her bedroom desk, Candace jackhammered keys on her work laptop. Her cell buzzed. Still typing, she checked the caller. Why didn't Trigg give up and take the hint? Surely, Miss M passed along what she'd told her friend yesterday afternoon on the phone. *I'm all right, Miss Mildred. I need a few days to work out a problem. That's all. I'll explain everything once it's all worked out.* Miss M had respected her boundaries. Why couldn't Trigg? She had no idea what she'd say to him anyway. *As soon as I get this work project done, and get over myself, I'm flying to the other side of the world to be a missionary. Tra-la. God's call. My nightmare.*

A text blipped. Enough. The phone had to go. She reached for it and saw the text.

I'm miserable.

She put her hand to her forehead and closed her eyes. Her crisis shouldn't be Trigg's. She shut her work laptop and moved to the bed as she speed dialed his number.

As she sat cross-legged on the bedspread, he answered. "Finally."

"I'm sorry I've made you miserable. Did Miss Mildred tell you what I told her?"

"Yeah. Real informative. 'I have a problem.' I'd say a whopper from what I saw yesterday in church."

"I'm sorry." But apparently, mostly for herself. Was this how she'd want Trigg to treat her if he had a crisis?

"I've got fifteen minutes left on my lunch break," he said. "Please tell me what you're comfortable sharing."

I'm miserable sounded good. "It's a long story."

"I still have fourteen minutes left."

"Okay, you asked for it. When I was ten, not long after I came to live with Grammy, a missionary from Papua New Guinea spoke at church. She'd brought a ten-year-old Papuan orphan girl with her on the trip. Showing slides of the people in the village where she served, the missionary painted a picture of the needs of the Papuan people. I hoped Grammy would put a twenty-dollar bill in the plate for the special collection. At that age, I thought that was a lot of money. Anyway, the missionary said it was difficult for Bible translators to produce Bibles in Papua New Guinea because people from villages a kilometer apart speak entirely different languages. There are 850 to 1,000 languages in Papua New Guinea.

"Wow. The terrain must be mountainous between villages to prevent them from communicating with each other."

"Yes. Volcanic mountains, networks of rivers, swamplands, and water surrounding small islands create barriers between villages."

"Go on."

"The girl, Idesah, boldly responded to the missionary's prompting to speak to us. She said she envied that children could read in this country, but her people had no written language. The missionaries who learned their language told them about Jesus, but they had no Bibles. She said she was an excellent learner and had learned English from the missionaries quickly. But she hoped someday to read a Bible in her own language.

"Idesah sat next to me at the church potluck meal after the service. She told me how lucky I was to read books. I felt so sad for her. And guilty that I could read all the books in my school library if I wanted to.

"At the end of the meal she asked, 'Will you help my people?' I said I didn't know what I could do. Idesah took my hands in hers and prayed, 'Dear God, please show my new friend how she can help my people. We need her help so very much. Thank You, Jesus, for hearing my prayer. Amen.' Then she asked me again if I would help her people. I said, 'Yes.'"

Candace's eyes teared up and her throat ached. "I have feared all my life ... that God wanted me to go to Papua New Guinea ... and be a missionary there. It's not that I don't want to help people. I love checking on and spending time with Miss Mildred. But I dread going to PNG."

"The attention you've poured on Gram has brought the sparkle back in her eyes."

"She's done the same for me. Why can't I be a friend to the elderly in the United States?"

"Why can't you?"

"Because of my promise to Idesah. Back when I was ten, I thought if I saved my allowance and gave half of it to the mission collections at church, God would let me stay here. My hope hasn't changed. I send a third of my take-home pay to missions, earmarked for Papua New Guinea. But I sense God wants something more."

"So yesterday, you thought the missionary being at church was God's sign."

"Yes. I think He's telling me it's time to go." Her voice quivered. "I want to be obedient, but I don't want to go." She pulled the bed comforter aside and wiped her eyes on a corner of the sheet.

"You do know that every two years Esther Little comes to speak at our church."

"But what are the odds she'd come on one of the four Sundays I'm here?"

"There are other ways to serve without becoming a missionary. Have you researched the possibilities?"

"No, but I'll have to now."

"Candace, some people are given the gift of making money and giving. Giving is a very important gift for the church. Don't play down the importance of what you've been able to do since you were a child."

"But my motives haven't been very honorable. I hoped God wouldn't make me go to Papua New Guinea if I donated a portion of my salary to spread the gospel to PNG."

"Maybe God is nudging you to change your motives and embrace what you are doing for Papuans. If you'd stayed to hear Esther Little's talk, you'd have heard the amazing things happening for Bible translators. People like you are providing ground transportation vehicles and helicopters, computers, and other communication devices so people like Idesah can know the Lord."

She'd never thought what she did was anywhere near as important as what missionaries did. Idesah had never asked her to come to her country, only to help her people. "Maybe."

"I wish I could be there with you." His voice was husky.

That would only make her want to stay in the US more.

"I'll be all right." She scooted off the bed. "I'm throwing myself into my work and pouting now, but the Lord will see me through. I'll consider what you said, Trigg. And I'll check on Miss Mildred this afternoon."

"I'm praying for you. By the way, your coat is at Gram's house. Oops. My fifteen minutes are up, and I'll be here late. I'll call tomorrow morning."

***

Candace's eyelids drifted open. Sunshine seeped through every open space around her curtains, as if the sun refused to be banned from her room. Either her body cells hadn't awakened or this was what calmness felt like. So ... restful. Of course, her brain cells couldn't wait to ruin her peace.

Papua New Guinea.

Her heart kept its steady beat. Amazing. Its rhythm seemed to say, "All is well, all is well, all is well."

"Okay, Lord, I'm ready to become one of your ambassadors to PNG."

Here.

God sometimes spoke to her that way, a word passing through her mind. Like after Mom, Daddy, and Jules died, the words *you'll be fine* had floated through her thoughts.

What did *here* mean? She'd just told God she'd go to Papua New Guinea. Her heart skipped a beat, and she clamped her hand over her mouth. Maybe Trigg was right, and she wasn't necessarily called to live in PNG. *Lord, please, please confirm that* here *means serving on US soil.*

Her cell buzzed on the end table. Trigg. She pressed the screen and placed the phone to her ear. "Hello."

"Guess what?"

He sounded excited. "What?"

"After I got home last night, I spent two hours researching partnering opportunities with Papua New

Guinea. I exercised a lot of self-control in not calling you at 2 a.m."

She wanted to tell him about hearing God's *here* and that she could possibly serve in Richmond, but telling him would be irresponsible. She needed confirmation.

He went on. "You can do all kinds of missionary computer programming work that you can do right from the good ole USA. Some from your own home. You can be part of a worldwide network. Programmers are needed for accounting, information management, and communication, as well as Bible translation. Programmers help with developing surveys and creating libraries for Bible translators. Unfortunately, all the jobs I saw for people working from home were volunteer positions, which means no pay. But what job could be better for a rich, number-one, hotshot programmer such as yourself? You could volunteer part time. Or retire and volunteer full time. With your low-cost living, you could live a year off what you receive from selling your grandmother's house alone."

Hope seeped through her. The good news was she could stay in her apartment, live off her wealth, and program away for PNG. A dream come true. Of course, she needed confirmation from the Lord before she let loose hallelujahs. On the other hand, nowhere in his spiel had Trigg given the slightest hint he'd be any part of her awesome new experience. In fact, he'd ended his pitch with the word *alone*.

"Candace, are you there?"

"Wow, I didn't realize so many programming possibilities are available. Thanks for researching, Trigg."

"I thought you'd be more jazzed."

"Like you're chawing on leasing my house for Miss Mildred, I need to chaw on this whirlwind of new prospects."

***

Candace sat at her desk, staring at code on her laptop. She hadn't typed anything for a long time. Her mind wouldn't stay focused. The possibilities for a new career had come so fast she couldn't take it all in. After eighteen years fearing she'd have to live in PNG to be a missionary, the possibility that she could do anything else was like entertaining an alien.

She turned over the sheet of notes she'd taken in the conference call with her company clients and jotted

God's will "here" - stay In Richmond?

Passion in a man - relationship with Trigg?

Passion in job - program for PNG?

Passion in helping people - visit Miss M & elderly in Richmond

Passion in faith - God is talking to me

So, this was what hope felt like. Peace and hope. She was on a roll.

She perused her list. It looked like she was getting ahead of herself. Confirmation from God on what *here* meant and the level of Trigg's interest in her were still unknowns.

One thing was certain. She needed to complete her client's project this morning. A realtor was coming late this afternoon.

***

The programming project complete, Candace shut her work laptop and left her room. Time for sweet tea and maybe a quick visit with Miss M.

In the hallway, her gaze fell on Grammy's door. She halted. The realtor would want to see Grammy's room. New curtains for the room hung over the stair railing and a can of white baseboard paint rested beside her door. With PNG and Trigg issues still up in the air, she could hang curtains and paint. Take her mind off the issues and lessen any need to sit on Grammy's bed to mope and grieve.

Candace grasped the cold knob and turned it. The door stuck, and she gave it a shove.

Darkness.

She marched to the windows and raised shades. Light flooded the room. She turned and surveyed the room, waiting for grief to flood her body. But no housedress lay on the flowery bed comforter. No mystery novel lay opened on the bedside table. Nothing was out of place to make her think of Grammy's last moments.

Addison had been here. When?

Candace pulled her phone from her back pocket and sat on the bed.

She speed-dialed Addison's number.

"Hello, Candace."

"When did you come to Twisty Creek and put Grammy's things away?"

"Congratulations. You went into Grammy's room."

"When did you drive out here from Charlotte?"

"A couple of weeks after you closed the house. I needed to say my goodbyes."

"Oh." Why had she never sensed Addison's grief? Her cousin had remained so cheerful after Grammy's passing.

Addison took a breath. "I noticed you'd straightened up the house but couldn't deal with Grammy's room. Her door was closed. So, I went in and put her things away."

"Thank you. That helped. Sad feelings haven't overwhelmed me as I feared."

"Good. Let in the good memories. That's what I did."

"I will."

"Everything else going well?"

"Yes. A realtor's coming in a few hours." She'd update Addison on her job and love life when their direction was clear.

"I know selling Grammy's house is the right thing, but it makes me sad."

"Yeah." Candace's gaze settled on the mountain

view outside a window. "I promised Miss Mildred that I'd visit her. So I'll see the mountains, hills, and valley's again, but knowing other people live in Grammy's house will feel strange."

"I'm sure. Well, gotta go to a meeting at church. I'm glad you called, Candace. You seem peaceful. Bye."

Candace shoved her phone into her back pocket and ran her hands over the bedspread. She pictured Grammy and her lying on Grammy's bed during Candace's preteen years. Grammy had read books to her, giving the characters unique voices—the gruff voice of a crotchety old man, a melodious voice of a fairy godmother.

Her gaze dropped to the round braided rug. Grammy had bought men's suits cheap at thrift stores and made the rug from scraps she'd cut from the suits. The rug covered the large space at the end of Grammy's four-poster bed. She and Grammy had danced on the rug to songs on the radio. Who else would a shy preteen dance with? As Grammy danced, her hips jiggled. Candace chuckled.

Grammy's burgundy Bible lay on the bedside table next to the inoperative phone and her radio. Candace lifted the worn leather book. Mom and Daddy hadn't been churchgoers. She'd received her faith from Grammy and this old Bible.

Slips of papers marked places in its thin pages. She laid the book on her lap, and it flopped open to a place in Jeremiah, where a folded sheet of paper lay. She opened the paper.

Her eyes widened, but her heart stayed calm. How strange. The note inside was addressed to "Candace, my dear granddaughter." In Grammy's familiar script, she'd written no more than a few sentences before the words stopped mid-sentence, as if she'd received a telephone call.

Candace read: "I'm thinking of you today, wishing you were here. I hope your new job is going well, and you are making some friends at the company and in your apartment building. I wish you could have found a job closer to here, but at least you're within visiting distance. Speaking of here—"

Candace stared at the note and counted three occurrences of *here*, the last at the abrupt ending. Was this the Lord's confirmation? But *here* in Grammy's letter meant Twisty Creek. If she were to serve PNG from the US as a programmer, it made sense to work in someplace like Richmond, where the Internet was fast and cell service worked everywhere. Besides, Trigg was in Richmond.

She refolded the paper, stuck it between the pages in the Book of Jeremiah, and set the Bible back on the night table. "Lord, this doesn't make sense." He'd have to confirm His confirmation before she could believe He'd chosen Twisty Creek.

13

TRIGG'S EXPECTED CALL CAME EARLY
Wednesday. Candace wiped off the white paint on her
fingers with a rag and answered her cell.

"Are you still chawing?" He sounded upbeat.

"Are you?" He'd had longer to chaw on Miss
Mildred's living arrangements than she'd had on
mission programming prospects. And no need to tell
him about *here*. His opinion on what the word meant
might create more confusion. She'd let that polecat lie.

"I've decided Gram is going to be happy only in her
own home." His confident tone contained a hint of
excitement. "So, I'm going to get an estimate on
expanding the half bath downstairs to a handicap-
friendly full bath. I can easily convert the dining room
into a bedroom."

"I admit I agree with you."

"Good. I think all will work out well for Gram. But
thanks for your kind offer."

"You're welcome. I'll call my realtor tomorrow and
officially put this place on the market." She laid her
paintbrush across the mouth of the paint can. "Today,
I'm painting the baseboards you removed in the

upstairs bathroom, so they'll be ready to reinstall after Randy Barnett lays the tile."

"Great. Did you have breakfast with Gram this morning?"

"Yes. She made cheese and blueberry crepes."

"Yum. I need you to do something for me. Can you close up the paint can for about an hour?"

"Sure." What was Trigg up to?

"Would you please drive Gram to Brayden's house? It has to be this morning because he leaves for work after lunch."

"I can do that. What's up?"

"You'll see."

"You're as bad as Brayden."

"How's that?" His voice sounded guarded.

Was that a smidge of jealousy? A face-to-face about Trigg's intentions—friendship or something more— would sure be helpful. Maybe she'd have her confirmation about where *here* lay on a world map by the time he came this weekend. She was praying they'd need the face-to-face, that God had heard her cries for a husband and family.

She rubbed at a spot of paint on the floor with her shirttail. "Brayden wouldn't play twenty questions with me on where he was taking me on our sort-of date."

"Oh. Well, we don't have time to play twenty questions, and I'd give you bogus answers anyway. This is a surprise, Marge. Call me after you get to

Brayden's house."

"Whoa. Where does he live?"

"On Trinity Road in the little brick house across from Coach Baylor's old house."

"Okay. I'll leave within five minutes."

"Make it four." He hung up.

Candace hammered the lid onto the paint can, washed her hands, removed her painting shirt, combed her hair, exited the house, and climbed into her car in record time. Surely less than five minutes.

Miss M became blustery when Candace prodded her to hurry. But noon was approaching fast.

Candace held up Miss M's handbag. "I've got your purse."

As Miss M climbed into the car she huffed a breath and set her purse on her lap. "I look a sight."

"I do too. I've been painting."

"So what's all this rush about?" Miss M pulled down the visor and peered into the mirror. Her hair looked fine, but she smoothed her hand over her strands.

"I don't know." Candace backed the Fiesta out of the driveway.

"Well, who put you up to all this?"

"I'll give you twenty questions."

***

At Brayden's house, Candace parked on the road in front of Billie Jean's truck. A red sedan, which someone had backed up the inclined driveway, sat behind Brayden's truck. Who in the world did Trigg want Miss M and her to meet?

"Do you know who drives the red car, Miss Mildred?" Candace turned off the engine.

"I don't rightly recognize the vehicle."

They got out of the Fiesta and shut their doors.

Brayden exited his house and sauntered down half his driveway. Billie Jean followed him. "Good morning, ladies. Fine day for a drive." He grinned.

"Yes, a lovely day." Candace glanced toward Brayden's porch. No one else exited his house. "Time to tell us what's going on, Brayden."

"I need Miss Mildred up here."

Miss M's eyebrows rose. "What do you need me for?"

Brayden dangled car keys. "The car is an automatic like your old car, Miss Mildred. Come get in the driver's seat, and I'll go over where the turn signals, wipers, and light switches are."

Candace turned to Miss M. The woman's gape was as wide as hers. "Trigg bought Miss Mildred a car?"

"Yep. Billie Jean and I picked it up early this morning in Christiansburg."

Miss M lumbered up the driveway's incline to the red sedan her purse swinging on her arm. "Well, I'll be. She's a beauty."

Candace followed her.

Billie Jean came alongside Miss M. "It drives like a

dream, Miss Mildred." She and Candace shared smiles.

"The car's only two years old." Brayden ran his hand over the shiny hood.

Billie Jean unhooked her keys from a belt loop. "I need to run." She hugged Miss M, waved to the others, and jogged to her truck.

Miss M shifted her eyes from the red car to Billie Jean's descent. "Where's she off to in such a hurry?"

Brayden chuckled. "She's got a date."

Miss M and Candace rotated their heads toward Brayden.

"I know the guy. He's a good person who'll treat Billie Jean right."

Billie Jean's truck roared off.

Brayden handed Miss M the keys. "Candace, might be good if you follow her home on this first run."

"I'd be honored to follow her home." Trigg had kept his word. Too bad he couldn't see the look on Miss M's face— She whipped her cell from her jeans pocket and snapped several photos.

Once Miss M had clicked herself into her seatbelt and Brayden had pointed out the features essential for a safe drive, Miss M started the car.

Candace hustled to her Fiesta, turned it around in the road, and let the car idle until Miss Mildred drove out of the driveway. She waved to Brayden and followed Miss M for the two-mile drive home.

Oh no. She was supposed to call Trigg. The road was too windy to chance a call. Miss M was no snail as she maneuvered the curves. Trigg would have to wait.

Although he'd been set on his grandmother giving up driving, he'd listened to her—and to Candace. Trigg was the kind of man she wanted for a husband.

Candace followed the red sedan into Miss M's driveway.

She threw the gearshift into Park, got out, and jogged to Miss M's car. Miss M accepted her offered hand. "So, what do you think?"

"I feel like a new woman. Wait till I visit my friends in my new red car. And won't others be surprised when I show up at church and see folks in the grocery store? Have you called that grandson of mine yet?"

Candace dug her phone from her pocket. "No, but let's call him now." She speed-dialed his number.

He picked up. "Hi, I've been dying here."

"A new woman would like to talk to you." She handed Miss M her cell.

Miss M put the phone to her ear. "Sweetheart, I love it. She drives smoother than my last car." She listened a moment. "Yes, I'll wear my hearing aids." She listened. "You don't have to worry about me driving to North Carolina or anything like that." She listened. "All right, dear, here she is." She extended the cell to Candace. "When you finish, come inside for some lunch." She walked to her porch, a bounce in her steps.

"Hey. I wish you could see your grandmother. I'll send you the photos I took at Brayden's."

"Thanks. I'm feeling good myself."

"I guess so. You just earned hero status with two Twisty Creek women."

"Two, huh? I couldn't ask for more. Well actually, I could. Ask for more. Will you go out to dinner with me in Wytheville and then to the dance at the firehouse on Valentine's Day?"

Her heart did the two-step. "How are you going to do that? Isn't that on a Wednesday?"

"Yep. I'm covering for another pharmacist this weekend, but I'll arrive in Twisty Creek mid-afternoon Wednesday."

A whole week until she'd see him. But … for an authentic date with Trigg, she was willing to pay the price.

"I'd love to go out with you. I've never been on a Valentine's Day date."

"Not even with Ron?"

"Don. No, I never went on any special date with Don."

"Then we'll make this one extra special. I have to get to work. Talk to you tomorrow."

She pocketed her phone and leaned against Miss M's new car. "Lord, things are going so well with Trigg. Please confirm I can stay in the US. I've sent off for information on a couple of volunteer programing jobs I can do from any place. You know I'll work hard to help Idesah's people with the skills and assets You've already given me."

Here.

Her heart juddered.

***

Time crawled—today was only Friday. The rest of Wednesday and all day yesterday, Candace had tried to stay busy working on a new project from her company, performing cosmetic improvements to Grammy's house, and watching Randy Barnett tile her bathroom floor in neutral-colored porcelain squares. Yesterday, Brayden had taken pity on her and bought her lunch at the diner. Only strict discipline had prevented her from talking about Trigg the whole time. Then, due to another pharmacist's illness, Trigg had to work a double shift last night, and they'd only talked briefly.

She needed to be back in Richmond, where their relationship could grow at a normal pace.

"Not complaining, Lord. I'm aware, we'd have no relationship with me in PNG."

She'd received no further communication from above, but the upcoming date with Trigg and the for-sale sign in her yard fostered hope.

The doorbell rang. Candace left her bedroom desk and descended the stairs. The doorbell ding-donged again as she opened the door.

Miss M stood on the porch brandishing a newspaper section. "Good news."

Candace stood aside. "Come in and tell me all about it. I'll make some tea." This had to be good news if Miss M walked over to her house. She looked outside.

A red sedan sat in her driveway. She smiled and closed the door. Now that Miss M had wheels, she'd most likely have more visits from her friend.

They walked through the house to the kitchen.

Miss M planted the newspaper on the kitchen table and jabbed a finger on the want ad she'd circled in red ink. "A pharmacist position has opened up in Galax."

Candace glared at the ad. No. No way. What was going on? The solution to her happiness was so simple. She and Trigg belonged together. In Richmond. With high-speed internet service.

Miss M grabbed her arm. "You've got to help me, honey. If I show this to Trigg, he'll ignore it, like he's done before. But if you show it to him and talk it up, he'll listen to you. It's right for him. I feel it in my bones. Lauren is no longer a reason for him to stay in Richmond. His friends are here. His grandmother is here."

But Candace would be in Richmond. Why couldn't things go right for once? Just once?

"Will you show it to him?"

Surely, even if she showed Trigg the ad, he'd want to keep his Richmond job. The long drive every weekend, the job difficulties—after-hour phone calls and unplanned double shifts—wouldn't sway him to take the Galax job, would they?

"Yes, I'll show it to him."

Miss M put a hand to her chest. "Thank you, honey. Did you see it's a managerial position? That might be a promotion."

"But the pay is probably less compared to Richmond."

"Yes, but the cost of living is less here."

She couldn't sneak one by Miss M.

"Trigg needs to see the ad real soon. Can you do that scan thing and send it to him?"

How'd Miss M know about scanning? Candace had planned to show Trigg the ad when he arrived Wednesday. Give other applicants time to apply and set up interviews. Maybe the pharmacy would hire someone before Trigg had a chance to apply. But now …

"I probably can do that."

"What was that, dear? My ears are so bad."

"I can scan the ad and send it to him." She curbed a sigh.

"Good."

"Let me make us tea."

"I can't stay, honey. I have a pineapple upside-down cake in the oven. This morning, I drove to the store for a can of pineapple rings. I can't tell you how free I feel, Candace." She pressed her hand to the table and stood. "Well, I better get back to my cake. Will you come over for a slice later?"

"I wouldn't miss it. We're on for my lesson to make cranberry scones tomorrow, aren't we?" She'd go crazy if she were alone all day Saturday.

"Of course, dear." At the door, Miss M patted her

arm. "Thanks for sending Trigg the job ad."

If only the ad would disappear in cyberspace. Did a person dare pray for technical difficulties?

***

Saturday morning, Candace paced past her personal laptop on the new trendy coffee table delivered yesterday, along with the rest of the living room furniture. She'd connected the laptop to her printer. Now all she had to do was press Scan to send the ad document to her laptop and email it to Trigg.

Miss M would surely ask if she'd sent the ad to Trigg when Candace arrived for her cranberry scone lesson this afternoon. Besides that, it wasn't her business to try to control the outcome of someone else's life, even if it might affect her own. She already felt guilty that she hadn't sent the ad last night. She'd told Miss M she'd send it to Trigg, and that was what she was going to do.

Candace clicked on Scan, waited, then emailed the ad to Trigg with no greeting, sales pitch, or explanation. He'd see it on his phone in minutes.

For the rest of the morning, as she worked on wowing up her bedroom, her cell remained quiet. She checked to make sure she'd turned the sound on. She had.

She evaluated her progress on her room. House hunters could be looking at her house as soon as today. If only she had a couple of Mr. Alderman's paintings to adorn the blank walls. She'd hid the kitten painting in her bedroom closet. That one had hung on Candace's bedroom wall forever. And Grammy's living room painting depicting children cavorting with dogs rested in the downstairs hall closet.

She dusted the furniture. When she came to her cell on the vanity, she stared at the device. Why hadn't it rung? She checked her texts. No new ones.

Maybe, instead of her cell, Trigg was busy calling the ad's phone number.

***

Candace collected a grater and a cutting board while Miss M gathered the dry ingredients for scones. A vehicle rumbled near the house. Maybe Trigg hadn't called because he was on his way to Twisty Creek to surprise her and Miss M.

Her heart pattering, she stood and strode to a living room window. Brayden approached the front porch. As she moved to the door, his boots clomped against wood and the storm door squeaked.

She wrenched the door open, surprising him. "Hi. How'd you know we're about to bake cranberry scones?"

"I've got a sniffer like a hound dog." He wiped his boots on the porch mat and entered. "How does Miss Mildred like her car?"

"She's a new woman. I'm glad I can go back to Richmond knowing she has transportation."

He slipped his hands into his back pockets, "I saw your for-sale sign. When are you leaving?"

"Thursday, the day after Valentine's Day."

"You got a date for Valentine's Day?"

"I do."

He nodded. "Miss M is going to miss you."

"Ooh. Thanks for making me feel guilty. I plan to come back and visit her often."

"Not the same."

"Did she put you up to this? She's good at getting others to do the leg work when she wants something done."

"No. It's just the truth. And you want to hear another truth?"

"I'm not sure. I don't think I can handle much more guilt."

"Too bad. Candace, you've blossomed here. You should stay."

"Yoo-hoo!" Miss M called. "Where are you, Candace?"

Candace and Brayden smiled at each other. He gestured for her to go first.

Miss M measured flour into a large bowl. "There you are. Oh, hello, Brayden."

He removed his cowboy hat. "I was in the area and thought I'd stop by to see how you like your new car."

"I love it. It's easy to drive and park and get out of. Sit yourself down and have a piece of my pineapple upside-down cake."

"Wouldn't turn it down." He pulled out a chair and sat.

Miss M slid a piece of cake onto his plate, and he polished it off. "I best be going." He scooted back his chair. "Enjoy the rest of your day." He left.

Candace grated lemon peel for the zest while Miss M quartered butter patties. "Have you ever thought of coming to Richmond for a visit?"

"Why would I want to go there?"

"Lots of history, theaters, museums, and Trigg and me."

Miss M gave Candace a tender smile. "The last two on your list are the only ones that interest me."

"You might like it there."

"Trigg comes home and complains about how bad the Richmond traffic is, says road construction is everywhere, but it can't keep up with housing growth. That don't sound like something I'd like." Miss M stopped cutting. "Honey, when you get to be my age and love a place as much as I love these mountains and valleys, you pray no one will—" She wiped her hands on her apron. "Come with me."

Candace laid the grater next to the cutting board and followed Miss M to the mudroom and out the back door.

Miss M lifted her open hand. "How could I ever leave that? It's magnificent even in winter."

Acres of fields sprinkled with ponds led to rolling hills covered with firs, which led to mountains three layers deep, the taller ones dusted with snow.

Candace exhaled a breath, forming a white cloud. "You couldn't, no more than Grammy could. I see that now."

Miss M wrapped her arms around herself and scanned the view. "Lots of the young leave, but eventually many come home." She raised her face to the blue sky. "This place is in their blood."

Miss M belonged here. And maybe, so did her grandson. She scanned the view. A peace settled inside her. Perhaps, like many of the younger people from Twisty Creek, the place was in her blood too.

14

ONLY ONE MORE DAY. TRIGG would be here tomorrow. Miss M had invited her to go visiting friends in her new red car after church, but Candace didn't want to miss Trigg's call. Then when he phoned, he didn't mention the want ad. She sure didn't bring it up. God had been silent.

For the hundredth time, Candace stopped keying code and admired her red dress hanging on the closet door. She rose, unhooked the hanger, and held the dress to her body, then stood before the mirror attached to the back of her bedroom door. She'd wear her hair down and apply the curling iron early so the curls would relax before her first Valentine's Day date.

Yesterday, she and Miss M had driven to Christiansburg to shop. In a department store, she'd selected and tried on a long-sleeved beige dress and a light-blue, turtled-necked sheath. Each time she came out of the dressing room to model the dresses for Miss M, her friend pursed her lips and shook her head. As soon as she modeled the red dress Miss M had whipped off a rack, Miss M insisted it was the right one.

Miss M wouldn't let Candace buy new black flats.

No. Miss M latched onto sparkly two-and-a-half-inch red heels that showed Candace's toes. Shoes she'd probably never wear again. Then Miss M marched them to Cosmetics and bought with her own money red lipstick, and polish for Candace's exposed toes. The woman was on a roll. Like a mouse in a maze, she wound them through clothes racks and counters to Jewelry. There, her eyes so full of twinkles she could've been Cupid on Medicare, Miss M insisted Candace buy sparkling teardrop earrings.

Hopefully, Candace wouldn't feel like a gaudy human Valentine. The invisible woman in a red dress.

But, oh, the thin-strapped pencil dress with the gathered back that began halfway down her spine was gorgeous. Its hem reached just below her knees. Would Trigg like the most stylish dress she'd ever worn?

She hung the dress in her closet and closed the door. Out of sight, out of mind. She had code to complete before lunch with Miss M.

***

This was the day. Candace floated through the house to the laundry room. She yanked a T-shirt from the drier and folded it on the short folding table. Trigg would arrive around 4:00 p.m., four hours from now.

Work was impossible. She wanted to include emoji hearts in the code, because ... drumroll ... this was the day. Valentine's Day.

During Trigg's call last night, besides making it

through another hour-long conversation with no mention of the pharmacy's want ad, he'd suggested she stay through the weekend so they could spend time with Miss M and each other. A no brainer. Of course, she'd stay three extra days. She could keep Grammy's house clean a few more days, especially since no realtor and house hunters had yet chased her from it. She'd follow Trigg back to Richmond on Sunday—after they stopped for Chinese.

"Thank You, Lord, for leading me here to find my passions—a man and the promise of an exciting new job helping the Papuans."

She'd taken God's silence about going to PNG and His *here* message as His confirmation that she didn't have to go there to serve Idesah's people.

And now, washing clothes and packing up some of her stuff would give her more time with Trigg and Miss M.

In fact, she'd go over and invite herself to lunch with Miss M. She lifted the stack of still-warm folded shirts and headed for the kitchen. The magnificent mountains outside the back window caught her eye. She'd miss the mountains and all the rolling hills. The forecast called for a heavy snow tomorrow. At least she'd see Twisty Creek's fields, hills, and mountains covered with snow again before she left. And the roads should be cleared by Sunday.

She did a double take. What was that up next to the fence? It looked like her trashcan. The wind had been blowing hard last night while she talked to Trigg.

Her clean clothes packed into one of the suitcases, she rushed downstairs, out the back door, and to the runaway trashcan. Boy, was it cold. Where was her fairy godmother when she needed a velvety black coat to complete her ensemble for the evening? Her tan car coat would diminish the magic.

The can safely stored in the mudroom, she jogged to Miss M's back door, knocked, and entered. Of course Miss M didn't hear her. She continued on to the kitchen. Miss M bustled around with pots and pans, then stuck her head inside the refrigerator.

"Could a freezing woman join you for lunch?" Candace said loudly.

Miss M pulled her head out and closed the refrigerator door. "Of course." Not a happy tone.

On the center of the table sat a batch of cranberry scones.

"You made another batch of scones and iced the tops with red icing. Aww. For Valentine's Day."

"Yes." An ice-capped word.

Floorboards creaked from the front of the house.

"Trigg's home early?" Candace headed for the dining room.

"Yes, but—"

Miss M's warning was too late.

In all her natural born-beauty, Lauren wandered around the living room rug while she talked on her cell. Her dark hair, pulled away from her face in a

French braid, revealed rosy cheeks and sensuous lips. Arched eyebrows complemented her huge green eyes. A red sweater and skinny jeans covered all her perfect curves—perfectly.

Candace stood frozen in the entry between the dining room and the living room.

What was Lauren doing in Miss M's house? How did she get here? And how was Trigg's early arrival connected to those two facts?

Lauren glanced her way. She ended the call, pocketed her phone, and in one second, scanned Candace's body. "You must be Candy."

Candace stiffened. "Candace."

"Oh, sorry. Candace." She smiled, uncovering perfect white teeth. "Weren't we in freshman English together?"

No. Freshman algebra, sophomore history, junior science, and senior government. "Hi."

Lauren gestured toward the front door. "Trigg went out. But he should be back in a few minutes. Are you staying for lunch?"

"No. I was just leaving." Although the front door was a few steps away, she'd leave through the back door. She needed more information from Miss M than her cold attitude. "Bye."

In the kitchen, Miss M thumped down a fourth plate, her lips pursed in the way everyone knew she was displeased.

If Miss M was agitated, something very wrong was

going on.

"I'm not staying," Candace whispered loudly close to Miss M's ear. "What's going on?"

"How should I know? I'm just the grandmother." She gathered the fourth set of flatware, plunked the utensils onto the plate, and carried the plate to the kitchen counter.

Lauren appeared at the kitchen doorway.

Candace pointed at the Valentine scones. "Enjoy the scones. They're delicious." She covered the distance to the mudroom in two long steps.

Back inside her house, Candace paced the new red area rug. She was no dummy. Genuine first love trumped rebound love every time. Trigg had never suggested anything other than friendship. *Sometimes a man just wants to enjoy a woman's company.* She couldn't technically fault him.

She kicked the leather ottoman. But she could un-technically dislike him very much. That was a smidge short of ungodly hatred, if anyone wanted to know. When did he intend to tell her his change of plans for tonight?

She returned to pacing. He was such a sap. Lauren played his heartstrings like a pro. They'd be divorced in six months. And dear old Candy wouldn't be around to pick up the pieces. Not on her life.

Her cell buzzed in her pocket. She wrangled the device with thumb and finger but couldn't get the stupid thing out of her pocket. Gritting her teeth, she yanked it. It slipped out and flew to the sofa. Striking her knee on the coffee table, she made it to the phone as soon as it stopped buzzing. Trigg.

She rubbed her knee. Not in a million years would she have answered the phone anyway. If he planned to break their date, she'd make the task near impossible. She'd march upstairs and wrap her red dress in newspaper like a dead fish and leave it on Trigg's porch with a sticky note adhered to it saying, "You're not such a great catch."

She sank to the sofa. And covered her eyes with her hands. Tears soon drenched her fingers.

Someone rapped on the front door.

Candace wiped her face with the underside of her T-shirt, then stared at the door. So, he had the guts to break the date in person.

Banging rattled the door. Let him try to knock down her door.

The knob turned and the door opened. Oh.

She stood, waiting, her fists to her lips.

Trigg's head poked inside like a turtle's from its shell. "Candace?" He rotated his head, saw her, and opened the door wide. The tall hunk covered the distance between them, his strong jaw set. Would he take her into his arms and smother her fears in a kiss?

He stopped a yard short of her and crossed his arms over his chest. "What's gotten into you?"

Her jaw dropped. "What's gotten into me? How about *who* has gotten into your soon-to-be-inherited

house? Because Miss M will die if you marry Lauren."
Bad comeback. Bad. Bad. Bad.

"Let's leave Gram out of this. I'm tired of being
henpecked. From Gram, from the new pharmacist
technician at work who thinks the world revolves
around her schedule, from Lauren, who, yes, has
wanted to get back together, and now"—he whipped
up a hand—you." He anchored his hands on his hips
and stared at her. "I thought you were different."

That was probably the bad comeback he wished he
hadn't said.

His eyebrows narrowed. "Did either you or Gram
think to ask what Lauren is doing in my soon-to-be-
inherited house?" His blue eyes blazed.

She swallowed. "Why was Lauren in your house?"

"Thank you." He uncrossed his arms. "Yesterday,
Lauren called me at work and asked when I was going
home next. When I told her today, she asked if she
could catch a ride to visit her parents. She was at
Gram's house because her parents don't get home from
work until around six and she decided to catch up with
Gram over lunch. Of course, Gram's reception wasn't
one of her friendliest. So I left them to stare at each
other to find out why you left and won't answer your
phone."

Candace held his gaze. "You said Lauren wanted
you two back together. How about that?"

He took a step closer and pointed his finger so close
to her nose, she'd have to cross her eyes to see his

fingertip. "I will arrive at your door at six o'clock sharp. You and I will go to dinner at The Log House in Wytheville, sway together to The Yesteryear Band's '70s music at the firehouse, and then sit at your kitchen table"—he swung his arm so his finger pointed toward the kitchen—"and have a conversation about our future. Got that?"

She nodded.

He turned and stormed from the house.

15

CANDACE'S HAIR FELL OVER HER shoulder as she sat on the rocker and buckled on a red, sparkly high heel. If Trigg so much as blinked the wrong way, she'd run upstairs and change into her basic black dress and ballet flats.

The doorbell rang.

She stood, smoothed her dress, and tossed her head to send her hair flowing down her back. Taking a deep breath, she walked across the red carpet, then her two-and-a-half-inch heels clicked on the hardwood. She took in a breath and opened the door.

Trigg's mouth began to form a smile, then gaped.

She grabbed his coat sleeve and tugged. "Come in before you let the heat out of the house, and I freeze."

He entered and she closed the door behind him.

His trench coat partially covered black slacks. His dress shoes shone. A red tie peeked from the top opening in his coat. She had a Valentine's date with the most handsome man in the world.

Trigg circled around her, setting a teardrop earring swinging. He whistled. "Marge, you clean up real nice. Wow."

He scanned her from her flowing hair to her painted

red toes, twice, his gaze slowing down on her red lips like a car on a speed bump. Miss M was right. He was gaga.

She spread her arms. "Do I look like a human Valentine Day's card?"

He pointed at her. "You can send this human Valentine to my house any day of the year."

Tingles went up her spine. To distract him from her flaming cheeks, she grabbed her coat off the back of the rocker. "Shall we go?"

He took the tan car coat from her and held it for her. "I promised Gram I'd bring you over so she can see how you look."

"Miss Mildred is my fairy godmother. She's the one who waved her wand in several areas of the department store and outfitted me in this red dress and accessories."

"Who knew she was as interested in fashion as she is in GHTV."

Candace laughed. "I feel like it's prom night. Or at least, how I think such a night would feel. I didn't go to prom my junior or senior year."

He winked. "We'll make up for that tonight."

***

Inside Miss M's house, Trigg hung his and Candace's coats on the rack beside the door. They found Miss M in the kitchen washing her plate and glass from her supper. When she saw them, she clasped her hands together under her chin and smiled.

Candace performed a full rotation for Miss M. "Do you like what you created?"

Miss M waved her away. "I just helped you pick out a few things."

"I don't care who created this goddess. She's beautiful."

Trigg handed his phone to Miss M, and she snapped photos of the two together.

"Well, that should do it." She returned the phone to Trigg. "You two stop lollygagging and go. Have a wonderful time."

"You're retiring already, Gram?"

"It's been a long day."

Trigg and Candace took turns kissing Miss M's cheek. She left the kitchen, and the stairs creaked as she climbed to the second floor.

Trigg riffled through a kitchen drawer.

"What are you doing?"

"The light bulbs are out in the basement, but Gram always has a good supply of flashlights around the house. She said you wanted to spiff up your house with a couple of Granddaddy's paintings. I'll take you down to the basement to pick out what you want. Then I'll put them in the SUV so I can take them inside your house when I bring you home. That way you can hang them tomorrow." He extracted two flashlights and tested one. "Here's one for you"—he tested a second— "and one for me."

He opened the door to the basement next to the pantry. "I'll leave the door ajar so we have more light to direct us down the stairs." He dug below the iced scones on the plate and extracted one without icing.

"You'll ruin your supper, Trigg."

"It's been a long day for me too. Gram sleeps, I eat." He directed his flashlight into the black abyss. "I'll go first. Watch your step in those shoes." He clamped the scone between his teeth and grasped her hand.

They descended the stairs, their flashlight beams parting the darkness. Like Grammy's, the basement smelled musty.

He held her hand tighter. "Wash is las tep."

"I can't believe I understood what you said." The last step was higher off the floor than the distance between the other stairs.

Standing on concrete, Trigg released her hand and removed the scone from his mouth. He bit off a corner of the triangular pastry. "Granddaddy's paintings are in the room under the stairs."

Candace held on to Trigg's jacket and shuffled close behind him. She waved her flashlight beam around the room. They passed a front car bench that came from pre-bucket-seat days. Boxes lined the cement block walls and a tabletop leaned against a box. In the table's center were inlaid darker and lighter squares that formed a checkerboard.

They turned into an alcove. "I hope you're going to

buy light bulbs tomorrow. If you don't, I will. Wonder if Miss Mildred wanted to come down here for something. A flashlight beam wouldn't be enough light for her to see her way down the stairs safely."

"I don't think there's anything she wants down here. Besides, the last bulb went out before I came over to your house, when I flipped the switch to see if the lights worked."

"Figures."

"Yeah." Inside the small room, Trigg directed a beam toward a stack of canvases, some in frames, others bare. "Granddaddy's gallery."

Candace stood beside Trigg. "Wow. Look at them all." She directed her flashlight toward a painting. "That's the New River." A tall rock face bordered one side of the river. "I love that one." She shifted her beam. "Oh, look at that one of the mountains."

"For now, you probably should choose ones with frames. We can clean them up to look like new."

"Let's go with those two, then, and get out of this cavern. I wish had my coat."

"Here, hold my scone and flashlight." Trigg lifted the two framed paintings. "You're in charge of leading the way—"

The door to the basement shut with a solid clunk. A click followed the clunk. Someone had locked them in.

"Gram!"

Silence.

Trigg leaned the paintings against a box and

grabbed a flashlight from Candace. "Stay here." He strode to the stairs and climbed them two at a time. "Gram!"

He pounded the door, calling for Miss M.

After a few minutes, Trigg stopped beating on the door and shouting for Miss M. He descended the stairs. "I think Gram must have come down for something in the kitchen, thought we were gone but had left the basement door open for some reason. Because we were in Granddaddy's room, she probably didn't see anything but darkness."

He rested his chin on his fist. No doubt, thinking through their predicament. His shadow, formed from her flashlight's glow, ran from the floor and up one wall and made him look like The Thinker.

"Gram's hearing is so bad, she couldn't hear me, especially if she was halfway up the stairs by the time I reached the door. I'm positive she didn't have her hearing aids in."

Candace shivered. "Unfortunately, my cell is in my coat pocket."

"And, of course, my cell doesn't get reception in Twisty Creek, so I left it in my room. I bet Gram is watching TV in her room with the volume on high. Our only hope is that she looks out her window and sees my car in the driveway."

Candace rubbed her arms.

Trigg shrugged out of his suit jacket. "Give me the scone." He held the scone in his teeth and held up his jacket. She directed the flashlights into the sleeves as if they were her extended arms, and he raised the coat over her shoulders.

She returned his flashlight to him and clinched his jacket lapels together at her neck. "That's so much better. But how about you?"

"I'm fine." He spoke absentmindedly. "I could kick in the door."

"Oh my. There must be some other way."

"He looked at his watch." He faced Candace. "I'm sorry. I don't think there's any way we can make our seven o'clock dinner reservation. Unless we break down the door."

"Does the lock have a skeleton key?"

"I know where you're going. Knock out the key, and rake it under the door with a ruler or the like. Sorry. It's a deadbolt."

"The window." She directed a flashlight shaft at the transom-like window near the ceiling.

"Only you could fit through that window, and it would be tight. Do you really want to ruin your new dress?"

"So what do we do?"

"Well, until we have a better idea— Hold the scone."

She took the scone, and Trigg scooted a box in front of the car bench, then placed the tabletop on the box.

They were going to play checkers?

He approached her and lifted his hand as if he'd

dive it inside her bosom. "May I?"

She stepped back. "May you what?"

A lock of hair had fallen over his forehead. That and his withering look endeared him to her heart.

He tapped her hand clutching his coat lapels together. She let go, keeping an eye on his fingers. He opened one side of his coat and withdrew a handkerchief from the breast pocket.

With a flourish, he opened the handkerchief and held it up for her to see. "Your tablecloth, mademoiselle." He placed the cloth on the tabletop, then gathered the two flashlights and set them on end, shining their rays toward the ceiling. He extended his hand to her. "The scone, please."

She laughed and handed him the pastry. "You are one determined man. We will have our Valentine's Day dinner."

He broke the scone in half and set the halves on the handkerchief.

She eyed the car bench. "You don't think we'll tip over if we sit on that?" She pointed to the car seat.

He dropped to the bench and rocked back and forth. "It's steady enough." He extended his hand toward her. "Come, sit."

She sat next to him. He thanked God for their scone and asked if He would rescue them soon.

She stared at her scone half.

"I gave you the side I didn't put in my mouth, if you're worried about that."

"It's not that. It's freezing down here. Can we survive the whole night?"

"It's above freezing. Don't worry. I'll kick down the door if we can't think of some other way out."

She took a bite of her scone. Boy, she was hungry. "A scone has never tasted so good."

"Uh huh. I wish I'd grabbed two. And a carton of milk."

A flashlight flickered.

He turned off the other one. "We'd better save a flashlight to execute our brilliant idea for our escape—when we have one."

She shivered.

He put his arm around her shoulders. "Okay. It's time to talk."

Her heart fluttered. "Do I get an agenda?"

"Sure. Two. A relationship. Three. Gram. Four. Depending on Two, Richmond or here."

"What happened to One?"

"It's right here." His gaze dropped to her lips. The flashlight flickered. His fingers caressed her cheek, and he pressed his lips to hers in a tender kiss that warmed her to her toes. She leaned into him and kissed him back.

Oh my. Turn on the AC.

He pulled away, but not too far. "I forgot. Five. End the meeting with another kiss."

"I like the beginning and ending, but the middle agenda items have me a little worried."

"Two. I'm crazy about you, Marge. What do you say to that?"

She was blown away, that's what. Stay cool. "Crazy about me or Marge?"

He kissed her nose. "You, Candace."

"Why?"

"Do people usually have a list of why they fall for someone?"

"You could have any woman. I'm no one special. As you know, I've always felt invisible."

"You're not invisible to me." He shifted on the bench. "Okay. If you need a list, I'll give you one. We'll go with letters this time. A. You were there when I needed you. You're incredibly kind to my grandmother, who I love dearly. I believe you love her too. B. You're not like the rest of the women I've dated. You truly care about things like your word to the little girl in Papua New Guinea. And you love the Lord. C. You're a one-person person. You wouldn't date Brayden, when you and I were"—he performed a so-so gesture—"sort of dating. D. You're funny. E. You're beautiful. F. You're—"

She made a T with her hands. "Time out."

"Yes?"

"You'd better stop there, or I won't believe you."

"Let me just add I love this little freckle, right here." He kissed her cheek near her ear. "And your chameleon eyes fascinate me. Right now, they have a violet hue in the flashlight glow. Your hair is like soft flax. And you in that red dress ... well, let's say I never expected that. Need I go on?"

"No. You're embarrassing me."

"Do you like me enough to consider a steady relationship?"

"I've liked you steadily since my freshman year in high school."

"But do you seriously like me."

"The truth is, Felix, I think I love you."

He smiled. "Felix or me?"

"You."

"Why?"

She gave him a-matter-of-fact expression. "You're a hunk."

He threw his head back and laughed. "That is the worst reason to love me."

"Okay. Okay. You care about your grandmother. You helped Billie Jean when she needed a friend."

"How did you know about that?"

"A little cupid with gray hair told me."

He chuckled. "Go on."

"You gave your ex-girlfriend a ride—for the last time, if you know what's good for you. You make me smile. You're truly interested in my projects. You said, 'Hey, how're you doing,' when you passed me in the hall in my junior year—which is why I voted for you for homecoming king."

He chuckled, then enfolded her in his arms and kissed her. The flashlight died. The kiss continued.

Thank goodness.

He pulled away, then kissed her nose. "I think I love you too."

If only she could've seen his eyes when he said those words.

He chafed her hands between his. "Do we need light for the next agenda items?"

She snuggled against him. "I'm fine with dark."

"Three. Gram. Over the last few weeks, I've realized I want to come home and live with Gram as long as she's alive. I was so glad when you thought so too. But I thought we needed a face-to-face to truly talk about logistics."

"This is not exactly a face-to-face."

He turned on the backup flashlight and grinned.

She could look at his face forever. "Why'd you think I was in favor of you living in Twisty Creek?" Hadn't she hinted the opposite?

"When I got your ad about the job here, I knew you agreed with what I thought I should do."

She formed another T.

"Go ahead."

"Miss Mildred asked me to send you the ad. I didn't want to. I wanted you in Richmond with me."

"Really. So you're serious about that for-sale sign in your yard? You weren't considering living in your house and working for a mission group here?"

Here. Oh, Lord, is that my confirmation? You truly want me to live here—next door to Trigg? And Miss

M? Her eyes grew damp.

He gave her a little shake. "Talk to me, because I applied for the job, did a phone interview, and got the position, at a pay cut, I might add."

"You're kidding."

"No, I'm not."

"On the day you told me about your research into the programming jobs I could do from home, I heard God say one word. Here. I thought, and hoped, he meant I was to stay in the US." She captured his gaze, frowning. "Do you know how many times people end sentences with the word *here?*"

He shook his head.

"Too many. And you just said it now. I think I'm supposed to live here."

He brushed aside a wisp of her hair. "Good. You had me worried."

"I think we covered Four along with Three. I can't believe I was redecorating Grammy's house for myself. She'd be happy."

"I'm looking forward to buying a truck."

"Are you sure Miss Mildred and I were your true motives for coming home?"

"Mostly. I have to admit driving a truck around here was a gully-washer reason."

She smacked his arm.

"Forget trucks." He turned off the flashlight. "It's time for Five."

He ran his fingers up into the back of her mane,

pulled her head to him, and kissed her. She grabbed a handful of his hair and returned his fervor.

After several moments, she pulled away. Talk about finding her passion. "I think you'd better kick in the door."

He turned on the flashlight and stood. "First, may I have this dance?" He extended his hand.

Candace put her hand in his, and he pulled her to her feet.

She wrapped her jacket-clad arms around his neck. "Can you hum our song?"

He stepped her around the cement floor within the confines of the flashlight beam and hummed "Too Much Heaven."

He kissed her. "I amend my claim. I'm sure I love you and hope we're married by next Valentine's Day."

"I hope it's way before next Valentine's Day, because I'd sort of like you to move into the house next door.

"We can ask Gram's opinion on a wedding date."

As far as Miss M was concerned, tomorrow would work—if she had time to bake a wedding cake.

She rested her face against Trigg's dress shirt. His heartbeats lulled her. Life was so good. She could dance in Trigg's arms forever. She'd have to call Addison tomorrow and tell her she'd found her passion for a job, for helping Miss M and Papuans, and for a man. Here.

Click. Clunk. The door squeaked.

Trigg dashed for the stairs. "Gram, don't shut the door. We're here!"

Miss M stuck her head into the basement. "Oh, sweet heaven, you *are* down there!"

Candice hurried up the stairs, and she and Trigg stepped into the warm house.

Miss M closed the door. "How could I have locked you in the basement? I'll never forgive myself. I got up to go to the bathroom and saw your car out front, Trigg. I wondered why you'd come home before nine o'clock. Then I remembered the open basement door. You must of near froze. I'm so sorry, dears."

Candace put her hands on either side of Miss M's distressed face and looked into her eyes. "Miss Mildred, it was the most romantic supper I've ever eaten."

"Supper? What could you've possibly eaten down there?"

Candace removed her cold hands from Miss M's face, moved to the round table, and picked up a scone. We shared a scone Trigg pinched from the plate before we went down to look at his grandfather's paintings."

"You must be starved— Oh no. You're reservations at The Log House."

"No problem, Gram. I'm sure you can make us sandwiches before we leave for the dance at the firehouse. It's only seven-fifty. The dance starts at nine."

As Miss M moved toward the refrigerator, Trigg put

his arm around her shoulders. "I sure hope you weren't trying to get rid of me, because I accepted the pharmacist job in Galax."

Miss M's hands went to her cheeks, and she turned to face Trigg. "You're going to move in here?"

"Yep."

Miss M beamed.

Candace held up a finger. "Now, Miss Mildred, don't get too accustomed to having Trigg here. He'll stay with you until he moves to my house."

Miss M's hands fell to her chest. "You're getting married?"

"I have a ring."

"You do?" Miss M and Trigg spoke simultaneously.

Candace clicked her sparkling red heels to the living room rug and padded across it to the coat tree. The others followed. She dug into her coat pocket and produced her mood ring. She slipped it on her finger. "The perfect engagement ring, because every color means one thing, Gram. See." She held out her hand and looked at Trigg. "I love your grandson."

MISS MILDRED'S CRANBERRY SCONES

Makes 8 scones.

Ingredients

2 c all-purpose flour
¼ c packed light brown sugar
3 T white sugar
1 T baking powder
½ t salt
5 T cold butter cut in cubes
1 c Craisins®
1 T grated orange zest
½ c chopped pecans
¾ c half-and-half cream
1 egg

Instructions

Preheat oven to 375 degrees.

In a large bowl, combine flour, brown sugar, white sugar, baking powder, and salt. Cut in butter cubes with a knife. Mix in lightly, Craisins®, orange zest, and pecans.

In separate bowl, beat half-and-half cream and egg. Stirring with a rubber spatula, pour in a small amount half-and-half cream and egg mixture at a time into dry ingredients until dough forms. Knead 5 times, but don't over knead the dough. Place dough on a floured surface and shape into a 8" circle and cut into 8 wedges. Place wedges on a lightly greased baking sheet.

Bake until golden brown, about 20 minutes, or 25 minutes in high altitudes.

I hope you enjoyed reading *The Invisible Woman in a Red Dress*. If you did, I would appreciate a short review on Amazon. As author Mary Manner so aptly says, "Positive reviews and word-of-mouth recommendations honor an author while also helping fellow readers to find quality fiction to read."

Thank you!

If you'd like to receive information on new releases, please follow me here: https://www.amazon.com/Zoe-M-McCarthy/e/B00ODC1ZNW/.

Zoe can be reached at www.zoemmccarthy.com, where she blogs regularly.

Gift of the Magpie

1

Who in her right mind agreed to a January 2 book deadline, knowing she'd spend Christmas alone, holed up in her house hammering laptop keys?

From her desk, Amanda Larrowe stared out her living room picture window at two feet of pristine snow—thanks to a snowfall so rare in Virginia that none of Richmond's small snowplow squadron had made it to her neighborhood.

A loud rumble came from beyond her window view. Amanda half stood and leaned forward to look down the street.

A snowplow. "Hurray!"

A green moving van traveled in the plow's wake and parked in front of the empty Craftsman house across the street.

Well, huh. The owners had never staked a For Sale sign in the yard. Maybe they'd decided to rent the place. Strange that people would move in two days before Christmas.

Yeah. As bizarre as a middle school teacher desperately needing a break—that would be her—

slaving over her manuscript during the holiday.

The rental truck, a small-sized option, stopped far enough down the street that she couldn't see into the driver's window.

"Come on, new neighbor. Get out of the truck and show yourself."

The door opened, and a guy in jeans, a blue-and-green plaid flannel shirt, and work boots unfolded himself from the truck. Long and lean. Late twenties. Would a Mrs. Long-and-Lean emerge from the other side?

The guy walked to the back of the truck and raised the door. No one joined him there or high-stepped through snow up to the front porch. A single guy? Not bad. Not bad at—

Wait one southern minute. Amanda stood taller and leaned toward the window. It couldn't be. Not Cam Lancaster. But, boy, even with whiskers shadowing his jaw, he resembled her high school foe.

Amanda scrambled around her chair and across the rug, hit the hardwood floor in her wool socks, and slid to the hall coat closet. She groped behind her stack of scarves for her field glasses, then returned to the desk.

The guy had lowered the loading ramp. Binoculars to her eyes, she adjusted the lenses. Now, if he'd turn toward her again ... There. She had the guy's face framed.

She lowered the field glasses and sank into her chair. Wha ...? Where ...? Why ...?

Closing her gaping mouth, she stared at her laptop screen, barely registering the red-and-white candy canes performing the can-can in the screen saver.

Wasn't being alone for Christmas enough?

Cam, the one person in the entire world she never wanted to see again, could not live less than a hundred yards from her front door. What were the odds of such a disaster? She might as well go outside, bury herself under a snow bank, and freeze to death. Better than giving him a second chance at murdering her self-worth as he'd nearly done ten years ago.

***

Her elbow on the desk, Amanda rested her chin on her palm. She watched as Cam finished shoveling the sidewalk along the curb and the pathway to his porch. He rammed his snow shovel into the snow near the bottom step and strolled to the truck.

Although still lean, he was no longer the skinny teen she remembered. While he'd lifted shovels of snow, his shirt had hinted at decent biceps and pecs hidden beneath the flannel. His hair was shorter, but plenty of dark curls covered his head above his ears.

He unloaded boxes from the truck.

Someday, when they happened to check their mailboxes at the same time, would he recognize her? She shuddered. Would she need to disguise herself with scarves, floppy hats, and black sunglasses every time she stepped outside her house?

Her gaze dropped to her screen clock. She'd been

staring out the window for half an hour? She couldn't allow spying on Cam to cause her to miss her deadline.

Amanda collected her laptop and mug and relocated to the kitchen at the back of the house. She opened her laptop on the red Formica table, filled her mug with reheated homemade hot chocolate, and counted out five white mini marshmallows into the heavenly smelling cocoa.

She drew a chair out from the table, plucked a breakfast cereal flake from the round red plastic seat, tossed it into the sink, and sat. To think the idea of a productive day had been foremost in her mind when the flake escaped her bowl this morning. She held her fingers suspended over the laptop keys and stared at the screen.

Humph. Like she focused so much better in the kitchen. When Cam arrived, her character, Dalton Taylor, had been foraging for wild berries, and now the lost middle schooler was still searching for berries.

A looming deadline and an embarrassing Cam-encounter were serious business. Sure, in fifty years, she might view Cam moving in across the street as hilarious, but she needed help now. And God knew this. Thankfully. Perhaps God would keep her on task and, in His mercy, send Cam back west where his family had relocated.

Dingdong.

Oh no! Cam had seen her gawking at him through the binoculars and recognized her—even though she'd lost twenty pounds, her zit problem had cleared, corrective laser eye surgery had retired her full-time glasses, and her braces were history. Did he stand at her door, waiting to reminisce the torture he'd inflicted on her vulnerable self-esteem during their junior year in high school?

Her heart rate keeping pace with eighty oh-nos per minute, she crept to the kitchen doorway and peeked around the jamb. A brown UPS truck had joined her ice-blue VW bug in her short driveway.

Her heart rate eased, and her jelly legs carried her to the front door. As she opened the door for the first time since the snowstorm, snow that had drifted against the door fell across the threshold. The cold air blasted inside, carrying the amorphous scent of snow. The green rental truck was gone.

A red-nosed UPS man stood on the porch, holding a flat box in one hand and a cube-shaped one under his other arm. "I have a package for Amanda Larrowe."

"Yes, that's me." Mud from the guy's tires stained the snow in her driveway like chocolate sauce on a half- eaten vanilla sundae. And he'd created a trail of huge holes in the snow from his truck to the door. Her yard had lost its pristine perfection.

He held out the second package. "And this one's for the house across the street. The porch is slushy where someone has trampled it. I hate to leave it there to soak up snow. Would you deliver this package to your neighbor?"

"Exactly whose house?" As if she didn't know from his description.

He looked at the address label. "Camden Lancaster."

If she knew already, why did she feel like hyperventilating? "I—"

He stacked the packages and shoved them into her arms. "Thanks so much, miss. So many last-minute packages to deliver." He double-timed his escape from the porch. "Merry Christmas!"

A full-time writer and speaker, **Zoe M. McCarthy**, writes contemporary Christian romances involving tenderness and humor. Believing opposites distract, Zoe creates heroes and heroines who learn to embrace their differences. When she's not writing, Zoe enjoys her six grandchildren, teaching Bible studies, leading workshops on writing, knitting and crocheting shawls for a prayer shawl ministry, and canoeing. She lives with her husband in the Blue Ridge Mountains of Virginia.

Zoe can be reached at www.zoemmccarthy.com, where she blogs regularly.

More Titles by Zoe M. McCarthy

Gift of the Magpie

Calculated Risk

Coming in 2018
The Putting Green Whisperer

91499484R00124

Made in the USA
Columbia, SC
16 March 2018